How To
Stop Fighting
About Money
&Make
Some

Also by Adriane G. Berg

Moneythink
Your Kids, Your Money
Your Wealth-building Years

How To Stop Fighting About Money & Make Some

A Couple's Guide to Financial Success

ADRIANE G. BERG

NEWMARKET PRESS · NEW YORK

88 89 90   10 9 8 7 6 5 4 3 2 1   HC

88 89 90   10 9 8 7 6 5 4 3 2 1   PB

Library of Congress Cataloging-in-Publication Data
Berg, Adriane G. (Adriane Gilda) 1948–
How to stop fighting about money and make some; a couples'
guide to financial success / Adriane G. Berg.
p. cm.
Includes index.
ISBN 1-557-04012-5
1. Married people—Finance, Personal. I. Title.
HG179.B44 1988 332.024'0655—dc19 87-34801 CIP

QUANTITY PURCHASES
Companies, professional groups, clubs and other organizations
may qualify for special terms when ordering quantities of this ti-
tle. For information contact: Special Sales Dept., Newmarket
Press, 18 East 48th Street, New York, New York 10017, or call
(212) 832-3575.
Book design by Mina Greenstein
Manufactured in the United States of America
First Edition

For STUART BOCHNER,
my best friend and
most worthy opponent

Contents

Introduction

CLOSE your eyes and picture a couple fighting about money. Why are they fighting? Where are they fighting? Who won? I'll bet you visualized them arguing over the wife's overspending. The duel took place in the kitchen, and no one actually won. The wife "got off," so to speak, with a warning, only to have the same scenario repeated the next week.

Now close your eyes and picture your *own* money fights. Are they really like the one described above? I doubt it. Budgeting, overspending, lack of money in general are often just symptoms of much deeper money problems. The reason behind most fights is in fact not a money shortage at all, but ignorance and disorganization. Fuzzy goals, confusion over investment choices, fear of future insecurity, and blame over past mistakes are often central.

Take Gloria and Paul, for example. This hardworking middle-aged couple unexpectedly received $500,000 from the will of a distant relative. The perfect fantasy, right? Well, not at first. For two months, Gloria and Paul fought constantly about what to do with this sudden windfall. Not *all* the fights revolved around money per se. Some involved whether he would retire, others whether they should move to a better place. Their fourteen-year-old son had no college fund. How much of the money should be allocated to him?

Gloria tried to read prospectuses, magazines, and money books. She got more educated, but also more confused. Paul spoke with brokers, bankers, insurance agents. Everybody gave him different advice. What the couple didn't do was *talk to each other.* They had no organized view of their own goals. They were in great danger of either doing nothing, or doing too much and investing in "get rich quick" schemes. After all, if you have no destination, any road will take you there.

Once Gloria and Paul began to work with me, we discovered that the true problem was his desire to retire on the West Coast and her desire to build her burgeoning children's apparel business in New York. When the task was set to fulfill these long-term goals, the *role* that the money had to play in their lives became clearer.

Now the couple plans to purchase a $180,000 condominium on the coast of Oregon, paying $42,000 in down-payment and closing costs. Paul decided to take early retirement at age fifty-five and receive pension benefits. Gloria would continue her business interest and explore the viability of a mail-order operation that would give her the freedom to move after three years.

The money is to be invested for preservation of capital and tax-free income: $150,000 in a tax-free municipal bond fund; $100,000 in a single premium deferred annuity that allows income tax on earnings to be deferred until the couple uses the income; $50,000 in a real-estate-based limited partnership structured for tax-free growth in the first two years and then for income; $80,000 in a trust for their son, to mature when he reaches the age of eighteen; and $53,000 in blue-chip stocks (highly safe and conservative).

For those of you who are counting, the remaining $25,000 pays for two first-class trips, one to Kenya and the other to the Orient. Now that's planning! It's also a way to enhance a marriage.

The sad truth is that most American couples miss their chance at making big money because of emotional, not economic, reasons. In fact, if there's one thing I've learned during my financial career it's this: MONEY PROBLEMS HAVE VERY LITTLE TO DO WITH MONEY! Many of my clients are rich, yet they have money problems. Over the years, as the family prospers, the same money conflicts persist. Even long-time partners in marriage and finance experience feelings of hostility that have never been resolved or even explored. After fifty years of marriage they still fight about money. Even with very wealthy people, the money fights are similar. The fights may be more sophisticated, they may have more to do with luxuries than necessities, but the conflicts are essentially the same.

What's missing between the parties is *teamwork*. Making money together is harder than making money separately. Yet, separate accumulation of wealth can break couples up. Goals begin to diverge, careers compete, jealousies ensue. Often, much worry and pain is devoted to money concerns by one party, while the other is left out of important decisions. Even when one partner is financially successful and willing to share the wealth, this is not enough to keep the relationship strong. Of course, impoverished bliss, even if shared, is not the answer. Teamwork is the key.

Society *sees* you as a money team. Indeed, couples are financially isolated from the rest of the family in America today. Imagine going to your brother-in-law for economic help. It's just not done. As an estates attorney, I have known for years that vertical interdependence (economic support between generations) is not only unusual in our culture, it is practically taboo. Couples today are simply expected to break off from their parents and become independent economically as soon as they marry, whether they were educated about personal finance or not.

It's understandably hard for new couples to establish a good working relationship with each other from the start. Yet, if they do, they can't miss! The couple who invests $1,200 a year at 10 percent in an individual retirement account (IRA) from the date of their marriage at age twenty-five until the date of their retirement at age sixty-five will have amassed $1,030,970. This is without any other wealth from their residence, stock portfolio, etc. One would think that this was motivation enough to get started young and to keep going. But it's not, because *money problems and conflicts are only partially about money. They are also about how you feel.*

The need for both financial training and emotional understanding is apparent to me in every aspect of my work with couples. I am in the unique position of being disciplined in two fields that usually do not merge in a single professional career: I am both a family lawyer and a financial advisor. For sixteen years I have represented husbands and wives in hundreds of divorces. I have drawn hundreds of wills for older couples who have enjoyed decades of happy marriage. I have acted as matrimonial mediator and trained numerous mental health professionals in the area of divorce mediation.

Six years ago I studied for my stockbroker's license so that I could help my clients deal with their financial advisors. I learned that even after a divorce settlement the wife and sometimes the husband needed financial guidance. So did my estate-planning clients. Once a will or trust was drawn, they needed to know how to manage their money. In acting as financial advisor and reviewing the recommendations of others, I learned that decision making, data gathering, and money management in general could be a painful process. I designed many techniques for successfully coping with that process. Through writings and seminars on effective team money-making, I was invited to host a daily radio call-in show in New York City on financial planning. This, more than anything, has given me a glimpse into the private financial lives of thousands.

Whether you have extra money, too little money, or are just getting by, you'll probably find yourself in the pages of this book. I've written it for practical people who want to get ahead, who nevertheless fight about money. Or, perhaps worse, who just can't communicate. All couples have different spending, earning, and investing patterns. They also have different systems of dealing with the financial side of their relationship. Often the system breaks down or needs renovation. There is nothing wrong with this; in fact, it can be healthy and positive.

There is a field of organizational theory that says that conflict is a stepping stone to progress. The best managers, so the theory goes, can face conflict among their employees and staff and use them to take a step into the future. The complacent company is the one that will not grow from its mistakes.

I think this is true of couples as well. The conflicts you share can be used to learn about yourselves, and at the same time to unlearn patterns that get in the way of making money. Money conflicts are stimulating; the stimulant can result in wrecking a relationship or making it grow. It's up to you.

Recently, I was called in as a consultant to a divorce mediator for what was described as a special case. The problem, the mediator said, was that her clients ran a business together, and not only was the marriage breaking up but the business as well. My reaction to this was that it was *not* a special case but as common as marriage itself.

Every couple, when they divorce, is breaking up a business as well as a marriage. The economic unit, no matter how unstable, to which they are accustomed is each other. Their decision-making patterns regarding money have developed in concert. Once one sees the predictable and habitual patterns, one can interrupt them and go on to establish new ways of relating to money and each other.

This book is a solution manual designed to help couples get beyond their problems and making joint money decisions that really work for them. Chapter 1 reveals the attitudes and practical strategies that are key to successful team money-making. Chapter 2 helps you organize yourself so you can make financial decisions in a businesslike way. Chapter 3 looks at your associations with money both culturally and from your particular family environment and helps you identify your personal approach to money issues. Chapter 4 teaches you to keep a diary of when and how you fight about money, in order to examine how your financial picture is affected. Chapter 5 describes and illustrates some of the most common money syndromes that afflict couples, and discusses remedies. Chapter 6 presents methods of conflict resolution adapted for couples from many areas in the field of dispute resolution.

Chapter 7 contains the 10-step financial-planning method that I've developed during my seventeen years as a lawyer and financial counselor. It is a blueprint to help you stop fighting about money and make some. If you follow this 10-Step-Method, you will overcome the single most important stumbling block to financial prosperity: lack of a concrete game plan.

The elements of the 10-Step Method are:

- Record keeping
- Goal setting
- Determining cash flow
- Budgeting
- Investment planning
- Calculating net worth
- Handling credit
- Insurance
- Housing
- Tax planning

Finally, I conclude with answers to the most important questions couples ask about their money matters, so you can begin on a solid footing.

Eventually, the 10-Step Method will give you the feeling of security you need to handle money effectively. New patterns of investing, decision making, and financial control will emerge as a natural result of good planning. You will not need to think twice regarding where you will be making your decisions or when you will be sitting down to talk about long-term goals. Your techniques and strategies will be set and, perhaps for the first time, you will be able to see the future from a financial point of view.

By learning to plan you will experience a financial domino effect. Security leads to reduced anxiety, which in turn leads to less fighting and more appropriate financial action, such as saving or investing. Subsequently, as more money is made, more security is experienced, and the cycle continues as you and your partner become financially more stable and begin to prize your financial teamwork.

HOW TO USE THIS BOOK

This book contains many worksheets to help you gather financial data and examine your personal finance patterns, past and present. To use the book, read it through once *without* preparing any of the worksheets. As you read, jot down the financial information you'll need to eventually fill in the data sheets. If you don't have the information on hand, at least write down what documents you must locate to find it. In this way, once you've read the book you'll be ready to start. After you've read through the book once, gather the information and prepare yourself to actually complete the questionnaires and data sheets.

Another device you'll encounter often in this book is the Silent Survey. These help you explore your associations with money—past, present, and future—in an effort to identify where problems may be rooted. They force you to tell yourself, privately, how you really feel about money issues.

When a Silent Survey comes up, have your pencil ready. Take the survey separately from your partner so as not to influence each other. Answer the questions briefly without pondering them. Some questions will motivate you to write long explanations; that means the issue is particularly important to you.

WORK ALONE OR WORK TOGETHER?

Don't be frustrated if your partner does not want to work with you on this book. You might be better off working alone.

The best approach is a combination, where one of you gathers all the data and the other enters it into the forms or keeps the diaries. As you will soon find out, this book is interactive. That means there is a great deal for you to do, alone or together. Most important, for the time being, you must put your anger aside if your partner does not want to participate or help you at all.

Many of you will be reading this book on a recommendation from a friend, or because you found it browsing through a bookstore or your local library. You may not have set out with your partner as a couple to try to stop fighting about money and make some. This leaves you with the task of initiating the whole process. If your partner is not as enthusiastic as you about examining money issues, don't let the whole ballgame end there and then.

Follow the procedure yourself if you cannot get immediate cooperation. Remember, you have a chicken-and-egg problem. Because you haven't learned to stop fighting yet, and because you haven't learned to work together yet, it's very difficult to convince your partner to start working in a synchronized fashion with you. Pretty soon, however, you will probably be able to coopt your mate into taking action with you. In other words, you'll start to work together as soon as you can show results.

Some of you, on the other hand, will be buying this book in concert. You will be equally committed to the task of peaceful financial coexistence, or should I say profitable financial coexistence. If so, you may want to parcel out your tasks. Pick and choose between the jobs you wish to do. In the boardroom chapter you will learn how best to allocate the tasks, before you have to begin to do any.

A small number of you will want to do everything together. That's fine, but remember it is not necessary. There is nothing wrong with allocating data gathering on assets to one party and data gathering regarding income to another. There is nothing wrong with each of you doing everything. What is wrong is not being organized about it in the first place. The only way to make these important decisions on structuring your tasks is to do so in a businesslike fashion.

WHERE AND HOW FAST TO WORK

From the onset you must treat the money-making strategies in this book as serious business. Look around your house now and see where you want to headquarter your financial planning activities.

If you even tentatively decide that the den, the kitchen table, the living-room desk, or your home office is the right place, begin work with this book there. Even now, you might be best off reading this preliminary overview in your chosen boardroom area rather than in the bath or in bed. It is simply good training. Chapter 2, which discusses choosing boardroom location and managing your boardroom meeting, will give you the information you need to pick a space wisely that will work for you in the long term.

Another important decision that only you can make regarding financial planning is its pace. The 10-Step Method for making money that I present at the end of this book is possible only after you have learned to stop fighting about it. However, the ten steps can be taken through intensive work over a ten-day or two-week period, or more languidly over a year.

Only you know how quickly you want to "get your act together." Only you know how busy you are with other matters and the extent to which financial success is a priority to you. Many of you may be reading this book because of a special crisis or decision that has to be made immediately. Your questions may concern whether to buy a home, or whether to sell one. You may be having a child or sending one off to college. You might want to speed up the process because you have a very specific goal regarding which you must make decisions. Some of you may have serious marital problems because of your money fights and may be reading this book in conjunction with counseling and other therapeutic methods. If so, your work with this book may have to keep pace with other helping strategies.

As you use this book to improve your financial picture and your interpersonal relationships, remember that the goal is financial planning, not therapy. You may not feel one bit better about certain money issues, and you will most certainly lapse into old habits now and then. What will happen is that you will have more money and be more confident in your ability to manage it, and this, in turn, will create peace.

I

OUT OF THE BEDROOM AND INTO THE BOARDROOM

1

How Successful Couples Do It

I N my practice I have handled scores of divorces and drafted hundreds of wills. Both processes reveal much about the quality of financial teamwork of the couple. Yet, the former marks a failed relationship, the latter a long-term commitment to mutual financial protection.

Five years ago I represented a divorcing husband who had some years earlier invested and lost $25,000 in corn futures. His wife was unforgiving; the marriage was a disaster and divorce was imminent. Two years later I prepared an estate plan for a couple married for over fifty years. Remarkably, this husband, too, had invested and lost $25,000 in corn futures. Neither husband nor wife was happy about the situation, but they accepted it as an unfortunate event, and no fault was ascribed. The glaring difference in the two couples' adjustment to the same financial loss was made more apparent by the fact that both remained affluent and suffered little actual lifestyle change. The effect of the bad investment on their lives was *created* by them as a result of their attitudes toward money and each other.

In the case of the divorced couple, the husband had exercised all the control over the finances. The wife was highly resentful but played a grudgingly dutiful role, rearing five children and hosting executive parties. (Eventually, she ran away with an artist.) The husband's tyranny over money and the wife's hostile feelings about it were never explored. So when he made an investment mistake, she had the opportunity to seize on it as a subject for incessant nagging.

By contrast, the estate-planning clients had shared their financial joys and woes for a long time. Whatever happened, they were "in it together." The husband was an executive and the wife a homemaker; however, she kept control over her own accounts and was an equal partner in the family finances. When he made a bad investment, she took her share of blame for failing to help him make the right decision. Because she was influential, she too was responsible. In the end it was the attitudes, not the dollars, that made the difference.

The difference between the successful couple and the unsuccessful couple is more than their actions. It is more than the success of their investments. It is the spirit of the whole relationship and how they interact on a daily basis with respect to money. No spouse is in total accord with the other's money habits. We are all as individual in our thinking, dress, and tastes as we are about money. A dull world it would be if we agreed on all things at all times.

Let's first examine the successful couples, the ones that get along when it comes to money matters. These couples develop a pattern or style of handling money that both parties can tolerate. Then they live with it. And when something goes wrong, whether it's the loss of a job or $25,000 in corn futures, the experience can be processed and dealt with in the context of their usual relationship.

The ultimate goal for readers of this book should be to emulate mechanically the behavior of the successful money-making couple in their attitudes and procedures until it becomes instinctive or at least habitual. Now let's look at the inducers of success:

THE ATTITUDES

While there are many roads to success, both in relationships and in finance, I have found that there are four attitudes that are key to creating a successful money team. They are quite simple and at times seem almost obvious, yet are surprisingly difficult to achieve and maintain. They are, in order of importance:

Trust
Autonomy
Fair dealing
Prosperity

Each of these earmarks of success are present in every couple getting along well enough to stay together. I recently had lunch with a friend and colleague and discussed some of the material included in this book. I mentioned to her that while I knew many couples who made money together, I had never met a couple who never fought over money during the course of their relationship. She said to me, "Well, now you have! How would you like to hear about a couple who never fought about money, not once, in thirty-eight years of marriage?" I was so shocked, I wasn't sure that I *did* want to hear about it. But when she began to relate the nature of the relationship she and her husband had, it became clear to me that this couple was a living example of the four attitudes that I planned to explain to you.

She described a relationship in which both husband and wife earned money in completely different careers without competition with each other. They earned money unequally; sometimes he earned more and sometimes she earned more. Because he preferred to make the investment decisions, her husband gave her control of the family finances. Like most people, she found record-keeping tedious and occasionally wished the burden wasn't on her. However, she had long ago decided that it enhanced her power in the relationship, so she kept the role. In addition, whenever either spouse received a windfall, bonus, or other lump sum, it was considered to belong to both. It was set aside for the purpose of having fun, investing together, or meeting some long-range goals in which both were interested. Finally, it had been a long time since either of them had really wanted for money. They are both very achievement-oriented and had prospered through the years. The result was a couple who literally never fought about money.

Let's examine each of the four attitudes that bring a couple closer to financial success, and see why I list them in a specific order of importance.

Trust

First, of all the fundamental requirements of team money making, nothing stands out so sharply as the need for *mutual trust.* Making money is a business. Things must be taken care of, checks must be written, money must be deposited, decisions must be made. Suspicion regarding any major money-related issue can wreak havoc with the relationship and with the smooth conduct of business. If a husband suspects that a wife will uncaringly overspend, he soon learns to hide his true income. Soon she feels belittled and betrayed. She begins to skim from her budget to hide money away for her own protection. And so it goes, deeper and deeper, until the lack of trust becomes cancerous enough to kill the relationship.

Sometimes, lack of trust is less insidious. A wife who does not earn money may have a vague fear of exposing her private funds to her husband and may simply keep one small secret account. A husband who feels guilty about not wanting to share a particular bonus may lie about his need to use it for his business, when in fact he's made a speculative investment with it of which he knows his wife would never approve. These spotty incidents of distrust do not necessarily ruin a relationship. But they don't make for good team money management either.

Consider a case of distrust that deprived two elderly people of the freedom to travel and enjoy their senior years. A seventy-two-year-old client of mine, who had been married twice, was already in the twentieth year of her second marriage. However, to her it was still her "new marriage," and she was still testing the relationship. During the course of her first marriage she had accumulated several thousand dollars in bonds, the existence of which she had never revealed to her second husband. The bonds had matured many years ago and were not accumulating any further interest. My client was fearful of cashing in the bonds because she did not want to declare them on her income tax returns and disclose their existence to her second husband. I explained to her that the bonds were federally tax free and would not have to be declared, but she was worried about state or city tax. I begged her to cash in the bonds and reveal the situation so that she and her husband could afford to travel the way they had dreamed, before they were no longer physically able to do so.

Whether she believed her husband would have taken the money for his own purposes or whether she felt the need for "money under the mattress," I could never discern. Nevertheless, she never could be honest with her husband about her hidden nest egg. As a result, these two very likable people never did travel, and never did use the proceeds of the bonds.

Sometimes distrust breeds indifference. The husband who does not believe that his wife should know about the family finances, either because he doesn't trust her judgment or because he feels it would reduce his power, often forces the wife to cope with her secondary position through indifference toward money. Here she becomes the little lost lamb who can't quite understand anything about the family finances. This increases the husband's belief that he is right not to involve her in money matters. It is possible for all to go well throughout the couple's life, but it usually does not.

At some point the wife's resentment usually surfaces, especially if she begins to educate herself regarding finances and this threatens the balance of the relationship.

A totally trusting couple can truly have a wonderful time of it. For one thing they don't worry as much, because they have at least one person who can carry the ball if they are not around. For another, they need do much less work, since there is someone who can share the burden of coping with financial problems, issues, and decisions. Emotionally, of course, perfect trust is very liberating. There's a good deal of relief in not having to look over someone's shoulder and not thinking anyone is looking over yours. Fortunately, most couples who plan to stay together *do* trust each other.

As you will see in the last section of this book, the data- and fact-gathering exercises of the 10-Step Method provide at least a mechanical cure for a less-than-trusting relationship. Because my 10-Step Method includes so much financial discovery, it is very difficult to hide information. Record keeping, calculating net worth, determining cash flow, and budgeting cannot be accomplished without truthful and complete information.

Autonomy

The second most important attitude for success is *autonomy. Every teammate must feel that they have money of their own.* This may sound like a contradiction to what has been said about trusting. However, trust does not mean that one always shares. In fact, many of the most trusting partners do not know everything about their spouse's finances. Their spouse would be willing to tell them, but they are trusting enough and busy enough not to need to know every detail. I am often asked whether I believe that partners should have separate accounts, and the answer is yes, yes, yes. I have known couples who comingle their funds so thoroughly that they cannot even surprise one another with a gift. This is wrong. There is nothing like the freedom to buy yourself a coat or a dinner out, or even to make an investment with independent funds. Because each individual has a different investment personality, and since one partner may be more willing to take risks than the other, it's a wonderful feeling to buy those corn futures with money toward which the other party does not feel proprietary.

Fair Dealing

I list *fair dealing* as third in importance because it usually follows when there is trust and autonomy in a relationship. By fair dealing I mean that both parties have a sense of relative equality in the relationship and generally believe in sharing with each other the fruits of their good money management. It means that both can expect their financial needs to be met if things go well. Like my friend who shares her bonuses, it means that if good fortune smiles on one partner, the other will naturally benefit as well. It does not mean that when all the material things accumulated by each member of couple are counted, their net value is about equal. We all know the couple, relatively happy, sometimes exceedingly so, in which either the husband or the wife never buys a thing for himself or herself. The other party seems to enjoy lavish shopping trips and to sport a new piece of jewelry every six months. This does not necessarily mean that things are not fair. It may mean that one of the couple does not require or desire as many material things. On the other hand, if one party was prevented from fulfilling their desires because of the behavior of their partner, the inevitable result would be resentment.

Eventually the long-suffering underdog may have his or her day. The solution could be anything from divorce to a good poke in the nose. Of course, there are many lifelong victims of unfairness, but this need not be. The opposite of fair dealing, inequality, can be corrected.

Prioritizing and sharing is essential to reaching mutual goals in both spending and investing. Any couple that genuinely wishes

9

to stop fighting about money and make some is going to have to prioritize in a way that's acceptable to both members. Often the negotiations that accompany goal setting and budgeting bring into the relationship a fundamental fairness that becomes habitual.

Prosperity

The fourth and final attitude that prevails in a successful relationship is one of *prosperity*. I list it fourth because it is an elusive quality that often comes and goes even in the best relationships. In describing financial status, the word *prosperity* has a very special meaning. It is quite different from adjectives such as *wealthy, rich,* and *comfortable*. Those words have a connotation of having arrived. *Prosperous* has a connotation that is dynamic, of people doing better and better with time. *Prosperity* has a solid ring to it. It conjures up thoughts of growing businesses, secure mom-and-pop operations, old-fashioned values, and general feelings of well-being. I have found that it is more important for a couple to feel prosperous than to feel rich. It is more important for them to be optimistic and hopeful about the future than content about the present. In fact, many a wealthy couple I've counseled begin their most severe fighting over money when they had finally "made it" after years of struggle. Often it is the aspiring couple who can see new doors opening up for them in the future who are the happiest with their financial lot.

A couple can feel prosperous at any economic level, even the lowest. All it takes is hope, a belief in the future, and a few results. The attitude of prosperity itself is a great motivator to action. Without it there's a feeling of such doom and gloom that not much can really be accomplished.

If a couple is imbued with a sense of prosperity, they are likely to take the steps necessary to bring them closer to wealth. A heartwarming example is the story of two young clients of mine who wanted to own an inn in England. They already had a nice cooperative apartment in the New York metropolitan area and two high-pressured middle-level corporate jobs with accompanying salaries. They planned together and were good team money managers going along on a normal course for corporate employees. While they were not exactly wealthy, and had by no means "arrived," they always felt optimistic and prosperous.

One day, much to my surprise, they came to see me with the proposition of opening an inn. Before they became too old (they were thirty) they wanted to sell their cooperative apartment, have me advise them on how to withdraw from their corporate pension, and leave the country. At first I felt some responsibility to talk them out of such a foolish and rash notion. But soon I began to see that they had thought out the matter thoroughly. Not only was this something they wanted to do, but they had every belief that they would prosper through making this move. So, while all their colleagues were striving for more valuable and expensive residences, they were liquidating theirs. Today they have followed their plan to a charming inn in the warm-weather southern coast of England, and are—well—prospering.

These two clients of mine differ measurably from the corporate couple who drop out of the "rat race" ashamed and feeling like failures. But *what* is the difference? Only attitude. Fortunately nothing helps to enhance the feelings of prosperity better than actually making some money!

Silent Survey #1

Now that we have reviewed the four essential attitudes toward financial success, take note of how you and your mate stand with respect to them. You may get some surprising answers. Have your mate answer the questions separately from you. Then compare the answers.

Trust

Do I trust my mate, most of the time, some of the time, not a bit?

Do I identify more with my mother or my father when it comes to trustworthiness?

Is the parent I identify with more the one who controlled the money?

11

Was I taught to put money away in my own name?

Was I taught to hide assets from my spouse for my own protection? Have I done so?

What do I believe would be the consequences if my spouse discovered my hidden assets?

Do I believe that my spouse has hidden assets, and if so, are they significant? What leads me to believe this?

Am I uncomfortable with the fact that I have failed to disclose assets?

Am I uncomfortable with the thought that my spouse may have failed to disclose assets?

Am I fully aware of my spouse's income?

Have I made him or her fully aware of mine?

If the answer is no to either of the above, why do I think this has occurred?

Have I been vague or obscure about the facts of my future prospects (such as bonuses or inheritance)?

Have I done so because I don't want to share such bounty with my spouse, or because I believe my spouse would coopt what is rightfully mine, or is there some other reason?

Do I trust my spouse to make wise financial decisions?

Do I trust myself to make wise financial decisions?

Do I feel more secure when our decision making is joint?

Autonomy

Do I have guilt-free separate funds that I can manage on my own? Does my spouse?

Would my spouse be angry if I decided to set up such a separate fund? Would I be angry if he or she decided to do so?

Would I resent my spouse making some independent financial decisions, including investment and purchases with joint funds? Would he or she resent my doing so?

Would I resent my spouse making such independent decisions with funds earned or received solely by him or her?

Would he or she be resentful if I did so?

Fair Dealing

If I were about to receive a bonus, inheritance, or windfall, would I share the benefit of it? Would my spouse share with me?

Have we fought over past failures to share or consult?

Are most of my financial plans for the benefit of both my mate and myself?

Have I felt that my mate appropriately shares his bounty with me?

Do I feel a sense of relative equality in the spending portion of our financial planning? In the saving portion? In the earning portion?

Prosperity

Do I generally feel optimistic about our financial future?

Do I think my spouse feels optimistic?

Have we in fact done better financially this year than last? This year than five years ago? Two years ago?

THE PROCEDURES

The positive attitudes I have just described are only one side of the success story. With feelings of trust, fair dealing, autonomy, and prosperity, it's unlikely that the couple will have any serious fights over money; but they may never make any either. It is their habits, the procedures that they follow with respect to money that actually help to make some. Attitude is a state of being, procedures make it easier to take action, and ultimately only action leads to making money.

It's because there are certain *procedures* that can be followed to enhance your financial picture that success in money making can be achieved. This is so even if your personal relationship is not ideal at the moment, and even while work is being done toward

13

its improvement. You may hate to diet, you may struggle against the thought every minute of the day, but if you don't eat, you'll lose weight no matter how you feel about it. This is true of team money making as well. One need not iron out every detail of one's temperamental approach to money making before the financial picture is enhanced.

While many financially successful couples don't rate 100 percent on the attitude scale, they *all* follow certain procedural essentials, specifically:

Communication
Task allocation
Decision making

Whether they express it or not, successful team money makers treat personal finances as a business. They respect each other and the money tasks that must be performed. That does not mean that they like them. They know that a certain amount of vigilance is necessary so that tasks do not "fall between the cracks" of an otherwise busy lifestyle.

Communication

By communication I mean *exchanging information about immediate money transactions.* Both partners must know when the other has written a check, charged a credit card, paid a bill, or refused to pay a bill. Because of the sometimes crushing demands of our busy modern life, we often fail or even forget to transmit important financial information to our teammate. This causes confusion and ultimately fighting. Being overdrawn at the bank is not pleasant; even less pleasant is being blamed for irresponsibility. Perhaps you have resolved not to pay a bill because you got bad service or received defective merchandise. If your mate doesn't know about your complaint and pays that bill, you've probably lost all chance at satisfaction. In short, when it comes to immediate money matters, you've got to let the other guy know what's going on. It's difficult enough to control your credit practices, particularly when "plastic" is being used. It's almost impossible to do so when two people are charging on the same account without conferring with each other.

Now, this sort of communication need not be in purple prose. A quick note on a bulletin board, a mark on the cash flow calendar (see chapter 7), even a "Hi, honey, I wrote a hundred-dollar check today on the Bank of North Minnesota," will do. Not that I encourage a slapdash approach, but at the very least *say something!*

Division of Tasks

In chapter 7 you will find a record-keeping system that is the ultimate in intracouple communication regarding money. Use it. However, in order to use it, one or both of you is going to have to sit down and enter figures. This brings us to the second important procedure followed by the successful team money maker, division of tasks. There are innumerable money tasks in this complex world of financial planning; however, in terms of the kind of work they require, they fall into only a few categories. They are:

- **Standing in line.** This represents all the time-wasting, mindless money tasks with which we are all burdened, including standing on line at the bank or the motor vehicle bureau, cashing checks, making deposits, etc.
- **Paying bills.** This involves actually sitting down at your desk looking over the bills, being sure that the billers are correctly charging you, making out the checks, and mailing them.
- **Filling out forms.** There are numerous places, including this book, where your financial affairs require the filling out of forms. Even if this takes place infrequently, it can be a horror nevertheless, e.g., applying for loans, filling out your tax returns, applying for credit.
- **Filing.** The paper chase requires that we file receipts, can-

celed checks, paid bills, proof of tax deductions, W-2 forms, and so on.

- **Record keeping.** Akin to filing is producing workable records from the data in the file, e.g., net worth statements, cash flow calendars, liability statements.
- **Balancing the checkbook and determining credit-card usage.** Both these tasks require a grasp of what has actually been spent and from what fund the money has been taken, therefore they are very similar. Both tasks reveal the short-term cash and liability position of the couple.
- **Speaking to experts.** At some point in the year you ought to have at least a passing conversation with your accountant, perhaps your attorney (especially if you are doing estate planning). On a regular basis you may be speaking to your broker (a dirty job, but someone has to do it!).
- **Making claims.** Your personal finances may require you to negotiate with a third party, e.g., the insurance company, your landlord, your contractor, or some other person or institution against whom you have a financial claim or dispute.
- **Resisting demands.** The flip side of making claims is resisting demands made on you from salespeople, claimants, bill collectors. These occur more or less often in your life depending on how complicated your finances are and how you treat the importance of these demands.
- **Making decisions.** The ultimate task, of course, is making your investment decisions. This is so important that it will be looked at separately and really should not be a task that is divided but a task that is shared.

In this morass of detail, which neither of you really wishes to handle, how do you divide your tasks? Many money fights rage over poor task division, and many a resentful dependency is created by the spouse who has surrendered his or her share of the tasks and concomitantly his or her share of the financial power to the other spouse. Remember, as ye sow, so shall ye reap. In short, the person who does most of the work feels most powerful in the financial relationship.

There is one exception to this, and that is the nonworking spouse (usually the woman) who's given certain drudge tasks to do because it is presumed that she has more time (e.g., standing in line, filing, filling out forms). Frequently, negotiating with the outside world, amassing data, and taking care of the taxes is left for the breadwinner or the one winning the most bread (still usually the man). In such a case, while a good deal of task division falls on the shoulders of one of the teammates, that teammate may still not feel in control.

Tasks should not be divided on the basis of gender, nor should they be divided on the basis of who is powerful and who is weak. In fact, there are four very specific considerations in task division. They are: time, convenience, skill, and enjoyment.

Tasks do not have to be divided equally. That is usually unrealistic. One party frequently *does* have more time than the other. So be it. That party should handle as much of the time-consuming tasks as they can absorb. In other cases, the party with less time may find some of the tasks more convenient, for example, the husband who works on Wall Street and whose office is right near the bank. Grumble though he might, it is more convenient for him to wait on line to make a deposit than for his suburban wife to drive twenty minutes to the bank, even if on the surface it appears that she has more time. Some tasks require a modicum of skill. In today's world of calculators and computers, math phobia is no excuse. Nevertheless, you may wish to pay bills but not be the one to balance the checkbook. If waves of nausea come upon you every time you have to add or subtract, give the task to the other guy. This doesn't mean that you relinquish your right (and your responsibility) to know what's going on. Get the results at your next boardroom meeting, which we'll talk about in detail a little later. And then there's always the little thing called enjoyment. Some of you may like doing some of the tasks. Grab them. I even know someone who enjoys filing; he finds it therapeutic!

If you are feeling a little disorganized about task allocation use the chart below. As you can see, it has been divided by tasks and by the four elements that you should consider when dividing tasks. Under each of your names (here I use Joe and Jane), put down on a scale from 1 to 10 (1 being the lowest and 10 the highest) how you stand with respect to time, convenience, skill, and enjoyment on each item. Many of you will find it useful to make a more personal chart that lists very specific tasks, e.g., paying the cooperative maintenance bill on time every month, handling the

ALLOCATING TASKS

Task	Time		Convenience		Skill		Enjoyment	
	Joe	Jane	Joe	Jane	Joe	Jane	Joe	Jane
Standing in line								
Paying bills								
Filling out forms								
Filing								
Record keeping								
Balancing checkbook								
Speaking to experts								
Making claims								
Resisting demands								
Making decisions								

insurance claim made by your neighbor for his ceiling damage, keeping track of your housekeeper's phone use. Any task that has either been avoided for too long, or the subject of a fight, should be separately listed and analyzed. Someone should be elected to handle it.

At some point you may just have to compromise. If you are all equal on all four elements of task selection, just divide them up randomly and do them! The successful couple knows that it's one for all and all for one. No one is angry because he or she is doing more of the work. The couple are aware that there is a reason, a basis for the task division. After you complete this chart, you will be aware of it too. You may end up reallocating your work, and this may shake up your relationship a bit.

Consider the example of one young couple. He is a dentist and she a stockbroker (yes, we have money fights too) who could never get started with their financial plan. They came to see me three months in a row and never brought all the papers I needed to get started.

Because her occupation was in finance, it was she who always had all the money tasks on her shoulders. They had decided to turn over a new leaf when they made a financial plan, as many couples do. He was determined to take more interest in the family funds and she was determined to unburden herself of some of the tasks. The result was that neither of them got started.

By breaking their usual pattern to achieve greater "fairness," this couple was destroying a good working relationship. Actually, their old pattern made a lot of sense. She was more skilled and enjoyed the money tasks more than he. Furthermore, because she worked at a desk with personal computers and calculators handy, it was more convenient for her to take care of these things. What they needed was not task allocation but *task acceptance*. They were doing fine task-wise, but they just didn't know it. Where they went wrong was in communicating; he always felt that he was in the dark, and she felt she had no one to talk to with regard to their money matters. Once this became clear, they brought in their material (written in her handwriting) and got going.

19

Remember, good money management is both a practical *and* an emotional endeavor. They go hand in hand. As money management improves, feelings about money improve as well, and vice-versa. Don't expect too much too soon. At this early stage try to avoid the task "power play." If you feel that you are doing a little too much and can't get your spouse to consent to do more, bite the bullet and do the extra work. On the other hand, if you feel that you have too few responsibilities, let the other guy do the work but insist on knowing what's going on through the boardroom-meeting technique described in the next chapter.

For most people task division is not a shattering issue. What it entails is the adoption of new habits. This is tough enough. Like eating right, or getting daily exercise, changing your money habits is something that evolves over time, since your bad habits took you a lifetime to acquire. Many of you may find that neither of you is paying the bills on any regular basis, no one wants to wait on line, and anyone with half a claim against you can get you to settle out of court in a minute because you don't want to face the hassle. If this is the case, you are both going to have to invoke a certain amount of will power.

Decision Making

The third and ultimately most important feature of the successful money couple is that they make decisions and act on them. The road to living on a measly Social Security stipend is paved with good intentions that have never been implemented. The problem with couples who fight about money is that they befuddle the financial issue so much they never draw a conclusion and can never take a step forward. This whole book is geared to working through that bind.

Once you get the hang of the 10-Step Method, you will be able to make decisions more easily. You will know whether to buy a stock or a bond, whether to fund your IRA or put a down payment on a new car. The beauty of the system is that the decisions make themselves. Eventually the couple becomes more instinctive about what's right for them financially, and their decisions can be less conservative and thus more financially exciting. For now, remember that decision making and its implementation is the name of the game.

Some of you will find that you make decisions and act on them, but not as a couple. This is a very serious team money-making issue. It means that there is some fundamental inequality in the relationship that is causing resentment and not resulting in the best financial decision making.

Successful money couples do not make every decision together. Yet, there is no feeling of inequality. Why? Attitude, again, is the answer. The party who is not the decision maker has voluntarily delegated responsibility rather than having it taken away. Remember that decision making is a task; it is listed in the chart on allocation of tasks. It may best be handled by the person with more time, skill, convenience, or enjoyment. For example, in my home decisions regarding our pension are made by me in conjunction with my office. This is only reasonable, because my husband is a labor lawyer. However, I have never actually put through a trade without informing him of my decision first. True, I would be surprised if he questioned it, but he can if he wants to. By delegating responsibility in decision making, one always has the privilege of taking it back. Once again, it is the attitude of trust and fair dealing that makes even one-sided decision making work.

Of course, there will always be some decisions on which you truly cannot agree. This may be caused by money personality conflicts or differences in priorities. The next chapter will help you identify where you may have decision-making problems, but for now, take another silent survey to put things in perspective:

Silent Survey #2

The three most urgent money decisions that we haven't made are:

The reasons we haven't made these decisions (number in order of importance) are:

__We fear making a mistake
__We don't have enough information to make the decision
__Our priorities differ and we've come to different conclusions
__The objective that we wish to achieve is obscure
__We are involved in a power struggle over decision making
__Other

One of the best decisions we've made regarding money is:
The decision was made together; separately; by one of us independently; by one of us with the knowledge and consent of the other.
The reason that the decision was good was we got lucky; we had a lot of information; we instinctively knew it was right; we had done the same thing before and it worked.
A poor financial decision that we've made in the past concerned:
The decision was made by both of us; one of us; one of us with the knowledge and consent of the other; both of us independently.
The problem with the decision was:
This happened because we had bad luck; we didn't know enough about what we were doing; we acted too conservatively; we took too much risk; our objective was obscure.

For better or worse, financial decision making brings you into a world without magic. The more I learn about money, the more I understand that personal finance is more of a science than an art. Most money decisions are either not made, or made incorrectly because of lack of information. Plain, simple, and mundane. One of the worst myths about money is that the other guy is brilliant and shrewd, and if only you knew what he knew, things would be different. That's just not so. As I've often said before in my books and articles, *the only real money problem is the ignorance of it.*

It is amazing how beneficial a hard-core grasp of your goals and personal financial picture can be in helping you not only make money decisions but make the right ones. Successful couples know a lot about their own money. There is no magic that makes them different from you, except that they pay attention. They treat money as a business and not as a burden. To do this they practice what I have called the boardroom method of money management. It creates a setting in which proper money decisions can be made and immediate action can be taken. Whether it's a decision regarding whether to pay a delinquent bill, or one concerning when to retire, they must be made in a boardroom atmosphere. We'll look at this important practice in the next chapter.

2

How to Run a Boardroom Meeting

NOBODY should plan a budget while riding in a car. That seems obvious. Nevertheless, more budgets are discussed under those circumstances or in the midst of meals than at any other time. Clearly these are the wrong circumstances for active money management.

Recently I witnessed the quintessential team money management mistake. My husband and I were in a movie theatre. Behind us was a young couple, polite and quiet throughout the movie. But at a crucial point toward the end, we heard the woman whisper loudly, "So, should we buy a co-op or a condominium?"

Where was her mind during this movie? Certainly not on the plot. And why should it be? She had been used to talking about important money matters any old place. What did she expect her husband to do, cry out, "Is there a broker in the house?" This is what I call keeping money matters in the bedroom.

I'm using the word *bedroom* symbolically, of course. I mean by it an inappropriate place: a place where money matters cannot be resolved; a place where people cannot efficiently make the best use of all the information they have; a place where the impact of other stimuli are ever present; and, finally, a place where all the other problems and conflicts of the team are most likely to develop.

As a divorce mediator, I know how carefully mediation rooms are furnished, how seating arrangements are changed to diffuse one-sided control and give a feeling of equality. As a stockbroker, I know how carefully meeting rooms are furnished, and the thought given to where the chairman of the board should sit. Environment is a symbol—nonverbal, but understood—that must be molded to the purpose of the activity taking place. The bedroom is not the place to resolve money matters; the bedroom is the place to fight about them.

Team money management must be taken out of the bedroom and brought to the boardroom. This is an essential secret. There is no point in doing anything else. Moreover, a boardroom rather than a bedroom mentality must be learned and applied. Everything in this book is designed to make the transition simple, welcome, and, most of all, lucrative.

The word *boardroom* I also use symbolically to mean a place and time that have been carved out from all other activities to devote to team money management. Information has been gathered, a presentation has been prepared, and all the good techniques used at successful business meetings have been applied by the couple. The more the couple suffers from a negative money syndrome, the more they will be helped by the boardroom atmosphere.

Getting started is by far the hardest thing you'll ever do. Note the advice of eminent family therapist Dr. Jürg Willi, in *Couples in Collusion*.

A man might run a business with his wife and live beyond his means leaving the accounts in disorder. He forces his wife to control him and

keep a check on him all the time. He thus threatens her with becoming even more careless. In reality he hates himself for his lack of will
power. The conflict will be resolved only when he is willing to manage his finances himself.[1]

Since participation in a boardroom meeting gives such a man the
power to have a say in his own finances, his old pattern of behavior is being pulled out from under him. He may act even more
careless and more helpless at the beginning just to hold on to his
old patterns. Beware of this, and don't despair.

Be forewarned that in taking matters of personal finance out of
the bedroom and bringing them into the boardroom, you will
probably suffer growing pains. You are changing your habits, perhaps even your way of thinking. If you've had a long relationship,
this won't be easy. Expect to slip back once in a while into bad
habits. For example, you may get organized enough to run three
or four boardroom meetings and then find that it's vacation time.
After you return you may have to reorganize all over again. It's
not much different from reintegrating yourself into work life. You
have to resume a routine. Actually, routine is what boardroom
meetings are all about. It means that you have changed your *mo-
dus operandi* with respect to personal finance.

Eventually, you will learn to keep all your material in one place,
to make your decisions in a particular room with your records on
hand, not to allow distractions (anything from children to television) to interfere with your financial discussions. In short, you
have given up the childish pleasure of being haphazard. Every
once in a while you may yearn for the good old days when you
could slap financial decisions together and hope for the best. The
best way to avoid such setbacks is to create the proper boardroom
atmosphere to begin with, the one that's most enjoyable to you,
the one that fits in best with your lifestyle.

To stop fighting about money and make some, you must conduct your joint money tasks and make your joint money decisions
at a boardroom meeting. Many of the boardroom principles also
apply to how you may want to conduct your separate tasks. For

27

example, if you have been designated the bill payer, you might want to use the same boardroom space with the handy tools and atmosphere you establish from your boardroom meetings. On the other hand, you may find it easier to pay your bills during your lunch hour at the office. In either case you have more flexibility with separate tasks.

It is the tasks and decisions that you must make together that require the boardroom meeting. To abandon your haphazard money style and embrace an effective, efficient procedure, you need to determine five variables for each boardroom meeting: its time, its place, the tools you'll need, the agenda, and the rules you will follow.

TIME

For many couples today, extra time may be harder to come by than extra money. Yet, you must set aside a specific period during which you are going to do joint tasks or make joint decisions. For many couples, disciplining themselves to take one full hour a week at the same time each week is the only way to proceed. (Think of it as financial therapy—you will be charged if you don't attend.) If you don't set aside this time, you may not see the money that you are losing immediately, but over the course of your lifetime together you'll be losing a fortune. Once again, attitude is important. Making money together must have at least enough priority to warrant your sitting down for a specific period of time on a regular basis. No one can tell you how much time you will need at first. But within a month you will be a great expert on how much time your financial affairs really take. You'll be surprised at how little time is needed once you've gotten your initial start. Please try to schedule your money meetings at peak energy times. If you are both "day" people, do your best to meet at lunch or use Saturday mornings.

For now, I suggest the weekly one- to two-hour meeting approach. I have found that most people cannot tolerate discussions of money matters for more than two hours at a shot, even in the office of a professional. In the early days I was willing to give clients any amount of time to accommodate them. After a while, I found that two hours was enough. Even the most ardent financial manager gets groggy and loses interest. Efficient decision-making and peak concentration take place in the first hour. But, at the beginning, don't rush things. Try not to limit yourself to a single hour.

Make a distinction in setting aside time for tasks and for decision making. If there are specific tasks you are planning to do together—for example, creating a budget—make the time relative to the task involved. If you feel you'll need a great deal of time, set aside three or four periods immediately. Make sure there is enough time set aside to complete the entire task. Don't get started and then believe that you will agree on a second session later on. This doesn't happen. More likely you will waste your first period by not finishing the task.

If you're setting aside time for a regular task that will be done routinely, isolate that task and meet for just that item. For example, if you plan to reconcile your checkbook together, do so once a week and do nothing else at that sitting. If you overload yourself, or expect to accomplish too much, you may find that the meeting never takes place.

To get started, take this Silent Survey #3.

Silent Survey #3

How much time do we need to set aside to perform a one-time major task, e.g., budgeting, creating a net worth statement, making a cash flow calendar?

How much time do we need to set aside for a constantly recurring financial maintenance task, e.g., reconciling our credit balance, balancing our checkbook, paying our bills?

How much time do we need to set aside for a highly technical task, e.g., preparing our tax returns, preparing to meet with our accountant, discussing the terms of our wills?

How much time do we need to set aside for long-term decision making, e.g., whom we should choose as our stockbroker, when we would like to retire, whether we want to move or stay put?

How much time do we need to set aside purely to make an investment decision, e.g., should we use an upcoming bonus to buy stocks or bonds? How we should invest this year's Keogh contribution? What should we do when our certificate of deposit matures?

How much time do we need to set aside for procedural decision-making, e.g., who starts a filing system, who fills out the charts in this book, how we will divide our tasks?

Once you have clearly focused on what you need to accomplish, the amount of time required will become more apparent. In addition to time for nonrecurring tasks, you should always have your weekly money meeting. Both periodic meetings and special meetings must be noted in your calendars in the office and at home. The key to the whole system is a businesslike approach. Just because it's "only" your spouse or mate doesn't mean you should feel free to disappoint them by missing meeting appointments.

There is probably no meeting of greater importance that you will attend during the week, from a financial point of view, than your own personal financial meeting. It's clear that wealth is built not merely from earnings but from what we do with our earnings. Just as you would not dream of missing a meeting with a potential new client because you could lose money, you should not dream of missing a meeting on your own personal finances because you surely will lose money.

Once you have set aside the time, make sure that you *will not be disturbed,* even if you must hire a babysitter for the period chosen or come home early from work while the kids are still in school. Make this time available. Successful money teammates do this automatically. The more organized they are, the more successful they become. Even those teammates who work almost entirely alone find that to be successful, they need a regular schedule to report to their spouse. They may not consciously make such a schedule, yet when I question them about their behavior I find that these autonomous and successful teammates adhere to a rather rigid procedure of communicating with their other half.

Remember that meetings are for the performance of tasks and the making of decisions. They are not for mere everyday transmittal of information. As discussed in the previous chapter under Communication, day-to-day information need not be shared ceremoniously. It can be transmitted with a note, a phone call, a message on a bulletin board, e.g., "I spent $500—check No. 738. Since you do the checkbook balancing, I wanted you to know about it. P.S. Don't forget to bring home potatoes."

PLACE AND TOOLS

Once the time has been set, the place must be chosen. This is easiest if done once and only once. While I use *boardroom* in the figurative sense, it's a great idea to have a space in your home or office at which your financial planning meetings always take place. This is convenient, avoids confusion, and allows you to stock the area with the tools that you will need for decision making. Without going deeply into interior design, it's evident that you'll want comfortable chairs (two of them), a sturdy table, a place for books and records, a small filing cabinet, and possibly a handy telephone—in short, as close to a home office as you can get. The following list comes from Stephanie Winston's excellent book, *Getting Organized.*

Postage scale (a small one) for oversized mail.
Rubber bands. Buy a small box of mixed sizes.
Rubber stamp and ink pad. This item is optional, but it is a nice idea. To eliminate the need for letterhead stationery, which is expensive, any office supply store can make up a stamp with your name and address.

Ruler.

Scissors.

Scratch paper. Buy some lined yellow pads for drafting letters and writing down thoughts.

Scotch tape and dispenser.

Stapler, staples, staple remover.

Stationery and envelopes. For most purposes 8 ½″ by 11″ plain white paper (with rag content for a better quality) and matching business-size (#10) envelopes are fine.

Telephone. You won't believe how much easier life will be if you install an extension right at your desk.

Typewriter.

Typewriter correction paper.

Wastebasket.

White-out fluid.

In addition, there are some truly helpful tools that should be kept at your boardroom location. Here is a list of items I have found invaluable in my financial planning practice that you should make an effort to obtain for yourself. It is amazing how these simple items allow you to operate on a wholly different level of professionalism with respect to your own financial planning:

Financial Planning Manual, published by Financial Planners Digest

Stock and bond stationery

Compound interest table (available at banks)

Copy of the Internal Revenue Code

Flexo-file or other expanding file system

The style of the boardroom and its location are entirely up to you. It may be anything from a separate room, a den, or the kitchen table if the things you need are available and the place is *quiet.* Whatever you do, take this space seriously. It may become one of the most important in your residence. And for heaven's sake, don't have only one comfortable chair. The person with the crummy chair always feels like a second-class citizen no matter what. Equality in money matters begins with equality in seating.

I have often known spouses who don't get their planning done because they are "too good a sport." For example, there's the oversized husband who willingly perches himself on the backless kitchen stool so his wife can have the single comfortable upholstered chair. Pretty soon this good sport stops coming to meetings; even he is not quite certain why. He thinks they are not doing any good, that things can be done more efficiently in a different way. A lot of his negative feelings stem from plain ordinary discomfort. So too the young wife who willingly sits cross-legged on the floor in her unfurnished living room while her husband is sprawled on the couch during boardroom sessions. This is simply no way to act. Don't minimize the importance of a decent chair, good overhead lighting, and sharp pencils. Once your location has been set, you probably won't have to set a new one until and unless you move.

AGENDA

Now you are ready to discuss the most frequently changing aspect of boardroom meetings: the agenda. Of course there will be a certain recurring agendas (the weekly meeting for filing, checkbook balancing, or whatever you have set for yourselves as joint tasks). However, there will also be special meetings. Think back to Silent Survey #2, where you listed the three most important financial decisions yet to be made. Start with these as your first agenda. This way, you'll get to the heart of the matter as quickly as possible.

Both parties must have equal right to call these meetings and equal right to set the agenda. The best way to call a special meeting is to use a financial planning bulletin board. An ordinary cork bulletin board with push pins, located in the general vicinity of the boardroom, will do. If something comes up, inform your mate that a meeting must be called. If there's unfinished business, set the agenda and date at the end of each boardroom meeting. But don't become a pest! If one of you is hungry for communication and feels that you have not had the chance to talk about money, you will set agendas left and right, post special notices of meetings, and generally gorge yourself on boardroom rendezvous. Naturally, this will soon make the other spouse wish to abandon the whole affair.

Proceed with the agenda as you would at any business meeting.

- Make a list of what you intend to accomplish.
- Place your goals in order of priority.
- Attack them one at a time.
- If time constraints don't permit you to finish, make a new date for completion.
- If the task is major, set several dates.

BOARDROOM RULES

Finally, you must set certain rules that enable you to "Bring the Adult into the Boardroom, and Keep Him or Her There." A boardroom meeting is an adult endeavor; the trick is to keep your interaction at an adult level. This is easier said than done. As an investment counselor, I have known couples who come seeking investment advice and degenerate into feuding children before my very eyes. As an estate planner, I have seen elderly couples married for upwards of fifty years who no longer even have to verbalize their feud. A pinch on the arm during a consultation, a look in the eye, a poke with the frame of a pair of glasses, tells the whole story. Yet, financial information must be applied in an atmosphere that's conducive to stop the fight over money and make some. In order for that to take place, certain rules must be established.

If your failure to make money as a couple stems from mere disorganization or lack of information, merely by going through the exercises in this book you will have solved many of your problems. The very boardroom atmosphere, with its readily available tools and structured format, will be enough to keep you on the right track.

However, if every time you sit down to balance your checkbook, you end up screaming at your husband about your mother-in-law's behavior, you know that you are going to need some extra help. Help comes in the form of the seven Cardinal Rules of Boardroom Behavior. The more you fight, the more strictly you must follow them. If necessary, print the rules on a large sign and hang it in the boardroom.

RULE ONE: Do not discuss anything but money at the boardroom meeting.

RULE TWO: Be sure to follow RULE ONE.

RULE THREE: Listen to what the other guy is saying; pretend it's a reading comprehension test and that you will be asked questions.

RULE FOUR: Take turns speaking.

RULE FIVE: Let the person with more information make a presentation divulging the information they have at the beginning of the meeting so that both parties are working from the same set of facts.

RULE SIX: Review the agenda and check off items as you have accomplished them.

RULE SEVEN: Never leave the meeting without another meeting set up and noted in your calendar.

In order to have your money make money, you have to work at it. It cannot be something that is comingled with all the tensions and distractions of the day. It cannot be inextricably intertwined with your emotions. That doesn't mean that you are not emotional about money; it just means that you are not going to act that way. To help you avoid this, let's take a look at where your feelings about money came from in the first place.

3

Understanding Your
Money Personality

THROUGHOUT this book you will have the opportunity to observe and analyze how you interact as a
money couple. In this chapter we will begin focusing on you *alone*
and your *own* personal psychology of money.

In my books on individual financial planning I spend a great
deal of time introducing the reader to his or her "money self."
Your past is important to your present, particularly in the area of
decision making, where there is a tendency to reenact your original family culture. When two partners' family cultures are in conflict, they fight.

Too often, there is an internal conflict between the parent in
you and the child in you. You may have a tendency to simulate
your parents' ways and repeat the responses you saw them make
in your childhood. It is the type of child we were and the parent

that we internalized that dictate the kind of money conflicts we are likely to have inside ourselves and with others.

YOUR MONEY CHILDHOOD

As I've already suggested, to find your money self, focus on what kind of money childhood you had.

In his book *The Psychonanalysis of Money*, Dr. Ernest Borneman begins by telling us that our toilet training often accounts for our view of money. He discusses the *anal* and *oral* personalities and how each type handles money differently. Differences range from going on spending binges to holding tight-fistedly to the loot. While I question the simplicity of such analysis, I do agree that the way we think about money is consolidated in our adult life, but is a very fundamental part of our childhood. So, instead of immediately analyzing your present budget, answer some of the following questions about yourself as a child:

Silent Survey #4

Did you get an allowance?

Was it too much or too little?

Did you think you were rich when you were growing up, or did you think you were poor? (Forget about what you really were.) What did you perceive yourself to be as you grew older?

Were you deprived of things like toys or movies?

What was happening in the world when you were a child?

Were you a Depression baby? Were you part of the baby boom, or did you come along later?

How did you compare to your friends? Were you all about equal in your allowance and toys, or were you in a poorer or richer crowd?

Did you ever move into a new money environment because your family suffered a financial disaster, or because your family was upwardly mobile? How did you react to the move in your childhood?

Were there discussions when you were a kid about whom you should marry? Did any of them revolve around money? Were you told to break a leg in front of a hospital so that you could marry a rich doctor? Did you believe it? Did you think marrying money was a goal you had to achieve to please your parents?

Was there a death in the family, creating a big gap in funds, or any financial upheaval?

Do you remember discussions between your parents about money? Did they fight about it all the time, or did it seem never to be an issue?

Well, you get the idea. Your particular style of worrying about money didn't come out of nowhere. If you reminisce about its sources (and I don't mean only for the time it takes to read this chapter), I guarantee that two things will happen. First, new revelations about your money attitudes will come to you. Second, you will get mighty uncomfortable. Few people in our society live through their childhood without some kind of money anxiety. It can rise out of a disaster like personal bankruptcy. As a child, you don't know what that means, but all the others in the family are whispering little secrets and passing on their worries to you. It can be caused by financial success as well: a parent gets a better job, but it means you have to move and leave your friends. Anxiety about money in one of my clients originated when a family member won the sweepstakes. The sudden windfall was greatly resented by the rest of the family. That memory had made my client fearful of taking risks because he might win!

This is not unusual. Money worries do not always stem from real money problems. I have said this before regarding ourselves as adults, and it is certainly true regarding ourselves as children. In her wonderful book, *Overcoming Your Fear of Success*, Dr. Martha Friedman points out that failure is sometimes a device to block something even more fearful—success.

It's not easy to separate yourself from your family money culture. Remember, we enjoy the patterns we bring with us, no matter how destructive or uncomfortable. We even enjoy our money fights as long as they are repetitious, unresolvable, and able to reconnect us with our childhood. To stop fighting about money and make some, you must drop your comfortable but fruitless patterns.

To learn more about the origins of your personal financial patterns, try visiting an amusement park. Make sure it is one that offers choices among souvenirs, candy, games, and rides. Don't go to a "one price covers all" place. Go where children or the adults with them must choose their enjoyments, where everything must be paid for separately.

Take your own kids, spouse, or a friend, and enjoy the trip. But while you are browsing around the amusement center, eavesdrop on all the children you can hear in the souvenir shops and near the rides. See how they ask their parents to buy them balloons, hear how the parents reply. Observe how the children react. Some will be making real choices, some will be given everything they wish, and others will be deprived altogether. Some will have their parents push toys or rides on them; other parents will obviously want to avoid spending anything. You will find that boys and girls are treated differently. Even twins will get different treatment.

I was struck recently by the behavior of two small children and their very serious-looking parents at a craft shop. The children wanted to buy something. Each had been given money and was expected to make a purchase. They had double pressure. They had to buy, and at the same time they had to buy within a dollar limit. Over and over again the children tested the parents to see if they would approve of a purchase before it was a final decision. The little girl saw a bell and asked the father, "I think that has value; does that have real value?" Depending on her father's reactions, she would like the bell and buy it or not. Neither child was making independent choices, for fear of parental disapproval. The basis of their choice would be value—not true value, their own value, but rather value in terms of how their parents saw it.

Some of your eavesdropping will be heartwarmingly positive. For example, one day on a bus I observed a little girl (perhaps four years old) with a package of M & M's candy. She asked her father, who had obviously bought it for her, how much it cost. The subject was raised by the child, not the father, who was paying the fare. The father explained to the little girl that the candy cost different amounts in different stores and gave her some prices. The girl looked at the candy, paused for a moment, looked up at her father, and said "Gee, I really appreciate this." It was a startling statement from a four-year old, and clearly heartfelt. The child was learning value through her own random experiences.

It doesn't really matter, though, whether your eavesdropping warms or curdles your heart. This isn't an exercise in passing judgment. What you are supposed to do at the amusement park is react, and see which of the many things you hear touches you personally. You will find someone whose thoughts about money as a little child remind you of yours. Instances from the past will come flooding back. If you have no reaction whatsoever, and it is not a result of your trying to hide your reactions, that too is highly significant. So far I have never met anyone who did not react to the assignment of eavesdropping in an amusement park. But if you have no recall whatsoever regarding your money personality, then you must conclude that some of your problems regarding positive, constructive, adult money handling may have to do with the loneliness it brings to you, since you have no childhood money past.

The amusement park exercise is a one-time quick means of immersing yourself in your own money background when you need fast results. There are hundreds of events around you, if you have more time, of which you can become aware. Did you collect for UNICEF? Have you had the experience of asking people for charity for others? For yourself? And, very important, did you work when you were a child and earn money? How old were you? How much did you earn? What did you do with it? How did you feel about earning money? Were you taught that hard work is best?

After you have reacquainted yourself with your money background, try to think objectively about the kind of adult you have become where personal finance is concerned. Remember that in the area of personal finance we are *expected* to transcend our family culture rather than merely emulate it. Nevertheless, economic realities may prevent this. This is particularly shattering for young people age thirty and under who feel they cannot do better than their parents financially. This often is depressing to them and robs them of the feeling of prosperity so important to financial harmony within couples.

Luckily you are likely to discover that you are not merely a repeat of your past. Most of us have come a long way. In answering the following Silent Survey #5, don't be unnecessarily negative. Many of us, particularly women, automatically assume we know nothing about money. There seems to be a safety in stated ignorance. Be truthful about how you feel about yourself, be objective about how you cope with adult financial matters. Later on, when you learn how to keep a diary about your fighting patterns (see chapter 4), you can correct any notions you may have about yourself as you analyze the actual day-to-day dynamics of your financial conduct.

Silent Survey #5

Reflect upon the following statements:

As an adult I feel in control about money/ disorganized about money.

I'm risk taking/ I'm conservative.

Whether risk taking or conservative, I am generally accepting of my investment personality/ I am nonaccepting.

I feel independent when it comes to money/ I feel dependent.

I am content with the material level I have reached/ I am discontent.

I feel secure financially/ I feel insecure.

I feel knowledgeable about money/ I feel ignorant about money.

Money is very important to me/ money is only moderately important to me.

I feel resentful when I must take care of my own money matters/ I feel healthy and powerful when I must take care of my own money matters.

When it comes to material things I would describe myself with three of the following adjectives: greedy, envious, charitable, generous, careless, acquisitive, frugal, cheap, extravagant, underprivileged.

In fact, others see me as:

My mate sees me as:

I am most contented with my financial ability to budget; make investments; find bargains.

I have real strength in the areas of:

I have greatest weaknesses in the areas of:

My keenest interest in money matters concerns:

I am least interested in the financial aspects of (stocks, bonds, real estate).

Now it's time to make some resolutions about yourself that will help you with money matters throughout this book and beyond.

- I will accept my tastes and abilities regarding money! (E.g., if I hate math I will get someone else to add—I will not give up on money management.)
- I will accept my basic consumer identity and work with it! (E.g., a monthly spending splurge will be part of my fixed budget expenses.)
- I will repeat the money successes I've had regardless of whether it fits into anyone else's pattern! (E.g., I will use my autonomous money to buy small tracts of raw land, even though my wife refuses to use joint money for a major investment; maybe she'll come around.)
- I will learn from my money mistakes.

43

- I will work with my investment personality and keep an open mind to new ideas!
- I will pursue my money strengths and devote time to learning and increasing them!
- As part of a team I will embrace my task-oriented strengths and offer to do them! (E.g., I will budget and pay bills.)
- I will banish the belief that money is for other people and that financial success can't happen to me!

Write down these resolutions and any additional ones personal to you and display them in your boardroom. Compare your resolutions with your teammate's. Where they coincide—both must forget the past or both hate math—work on these issues. (Don't bring up old hurts; resolve to buy a calculator and use it.) Where they are in conflict (you believe stocks are the best investment, he thinks real estate is the key to success), use the suggestions for conflict resolution found in chapter 6 to work out a money-making compromise.

THE JOYS OF BLAME AND THE REWARDS OF HELPLESSNESS

No discussion of finances and emotions would be complete without a discussion of the Tweedle-dum and Tweedle-dee of money fights: blame and helplessness. Usually the blaming spouse is also the one who has acted helplessly or has given up control over the financial situation. The blamed spouse is the one who has acted *aggressively* and perhaps has made a mistake that his money mate never lets him forget. Couples may take turns blaming each other and acting helplessly. After a while they can operate with exquisite precision to arouse each other into battles through patterns of blaming.

Worst of all, the blame-helplessness dynamic becomes a way of responding to a decision-making situation and avoiding decisions. Note the following analysis by psychoanalyst and couples counselor Dr. Jürg Willi:

> An endless battle will ensue as long as the husband represses any trace of weakness or passivity in himself and as long as the wife continues to identify with an extreme image of herself as a husband-worshipper.
> The fundamental cause of conflict, therefore, lies in both partners' resistance to confronting repressed layers of the personality, whether their own or the partner's. Moreover, refusal to confront the unconscious creates a sense of guilt which, projected upon the other, makes them appear responsible for one's own failure. "I am how I am only because you are like you are. If you were different, I would be different too." The other's poor performance serves as an alibi for the self's poor performance. The partners lock each other into a collusive circle of interaction.[2]

There are many types of blamer-blamee patterns. For example, in one type the blamer "passes the buck." This blamer escapes having to make any money decisions by imbuing the other with the power to make the final decision. The blamer feels (and acts) too dumb, too lazy, or too uncaring actually to make the decision. This type of blamer says, "I know nothing, I am stupid. You must do the job. Therefore, if we have any money problems it's your fault."

To keep up the pressure on the resented "powerful" mate, this blamer usually conjures up old mistakes ($25,000 lost in corn futures) to remind the blamee of how wrong they have been in the past. This virtually immobilizes the poor blamee, who no longer feels like making any new decisions. This, in turn, incites the blamer to further anger and gives more fuel to the argument that the blamed spouse is not carrying their share of the burden. Result: No one makes any money decisions.

Another type of blamer enjoys the *power* of the blaming act. Most of us first encounter blame as children when our parents yell at us. When we do this to another as an adult we have become the parent, the victor, the stronger of the two. As childish as blaming may be, there is a power in it that cannot escape notice. In particular the less powerful spouse may use blaming as a technique to seize the upper hand. The result of blaming for power is exactly the same as the result of pass-the-buck blaming. The other party does not want to take action, doesn't want to get yelled at, doesn't want to get blamed. Often, when it's the dependent spouse who does the blaming, the tone is one of helpless whining that even more enrages the blamed spouse.

Frequently, it is the more powerful spouse who blames the helpless spouse for every little infraction. This is a second situation in which blaming can equal power. Victim and victimizer usually end up making no decisions after their bang-up fight but merely reinforcing the powerful/powerless dynamic under which they are operating.

Finally, blame can revolve around a one-time hideous incident that one or both of the parties can never forget (corn futures again). Lately, because of the rapidly appreciating real estate market, houses, co-ops, and condominiums that one or both parties have passed up is the subject of much blame.

Silent Survey #6

Is there a specific money-related incident for which you cannot forgive your mate? For which you cannot be forgiven?

Is there a particular topic that comes up recurrently and is a constant sore point in your money discussions?

Do you find yourself bringing blame into the money-making decision process in a more general way?

Are you the blamer or the blamee?

Do the two of you take turns?

What is your spouse's reaction to your blame?

What is your reaction to his (hers)?

Is decision-making difficult because either or both fear reprisal?

If your spouse persists in attaching blame to a specific incident, the best thing you can do is shut up! A good method of keeping blame out of the boardroom is simply to resolve that there will be no talking about each other's failures during your boardroom meetings. If necessary, post a sign:

I WILL NOT MENTION YOUR PAST INVESTMENT MISTAKES.

I WILL NOT TALK ABOUT THE LOAN YOU MADE TO YOUR BROTHER-IN-LAW THREE YEARS AGO THAT HE NEVER PAID BACK.

THERE WILL BE NO TALKING ABOUT YOUR OVERSPENDING HABITS WHEN WE ARE DISCUSSING INVESTMENT ANALYSIS.

So much for Tweedle-dee. Now let's look at Tweedle-dum, the self-blamer or the helpless personality. This person, too, wishes to avoid decision making. Helplessness is a time-honored response to achievement avoidance. The self-blamer merely throws up his hands, proclaims ignorance, and makes no decision at all. The actual object of self-blame is to get the other teammate to take over the money tasks, to show love and affection, to be the nurturer and supporter. Once again, acknowledgment and identification of this dynamic is the best way for you to nip the tendency in the bud. Talking about how helpless and ignorant you are is not going to get a budget made, an investment decision completed, or a house purchased.

Silent Survey #7

Do I really believe that I am ignorant or is it just a comforting thought?

How does my spouse operate at work and in other settings, with responsibility or with dependence?

How can I improve my own knowledge so that I don't feel ignorant?

How will I feel about losing the excuse of ignorance and having to take responsibility for my own money?

How will I feel if I take a chance and make a financial decision and get blamed?

Ultimately it is not necessary to resolve all the emotional problems that relate to money. Identifying them may be enough, and working on the one or two that really seem to stand in the way of the decision-making process is usually all that's necessary for a major breakthrough. If all discussion regarding money dissolves into childish blame sessions, then this is obviously a significant trouble spot. If the egregious error is brought up once a year, forget about it, and work on something else.

LOVE AND MONEY

Several years ago I was asked to draft a prenuptial agreement for a woman of meager financial means who was about to marry a multimillionaire. Under the terms of that agreement he was to transfer to her immediately the sum of $1 million. In getting to know the couple I was assured that this was being done so that she would feel equal in the relationship and that he had no fear whatsoever that she was marrying him for his money or for this transfer.

However, no one in our offices believed that this woman was anything other than a gold-digger. Everyone expected that the marriage would eventually go sour and she would "make out like a bandit," as one attorney put it. In fact, they have been married for years and the marriage is stronger than ever.

While these people knew what they were doing, love and money are frequently confused. The confusion begins very early in life, when money is used for reward and punishment. "You're such a good boy today, I'm going to buy you a toy." "If you don't stop crying I'll take away your allowance and give you something to cry about." Women especially are taught that part of a man's love is taking care, and that taking care has become translated into materialism.

The fact is that almost everything in our society is measured in terms of monetary value, so why shouldn't the quality of our affection be measured that way as well? One of the few things that separates humans from animals is that humans measure their ability to survive in currency, whereas animals rely on self-sufficiency. Ever since human beings became more highly evolved, survival and currency have been intertwined, and the more dependent teammate (usually the woman) measures a man's love by his willingness to support her.

In more superficial ways, we reinforce these concepts. Every time a card manufacturer creates a special day—grandmother's day, dog's day, secretary's day—we feel compelled to bestow some material gift to show our love. Sometimes we can even practice this *quid pro quo* of love for money on ourselves: *I'll be good to myself today, I'll buy myself something!*

When one party in a relationship does not feel they are getting their fair share (whether or not they judge it realistically), they don't feel loved and become angry and resentful. Fighting is inevitable. Sometimes the deprivation is not in terms of direct material things; sometimes it's more subtle, such as the feeling that the future is not secure. When one teammate refuses to do long-range planning and the other feels needy with regard to coping with retirement or eventual college tuition or future housing, they may feel deprived, unloved, and therefore resentful even in the absence of any immediate effect on their day-to-day material welfare.

Silent Survey #8
Part I

Are the following statements true or false:

I do not believe my spouse is carrying his or her fair share of the income burden.

I feel materially deprived even though I believe my spouse has enough money.

I feel materially deprived and I am angry at my spouse because
  he (she) does not have enough money.
If my spouse loved me more I would get more.

Part II

Answer true or false:
I do not believe I am carrying my fair share of the income
  burden.
My mate gets fewer material things than I.
I sense my mate is angry at me because I get more.
If I loved my mate more I'd be more generous.

If you conclude that money is a measure of your teammate's
love for you, don't be surprised. You may be right! If your mate
is withholding money, being cheap, deliberately putting greater
burden on you to support the family, it is not ridiculous to conclude that there's a lack of caring in the picture. When we love
someone, we want to share with them. When we love them passionately, we want to give them everything. Many of us feel that
emotion most deeply with respect to our children. A parsimon-
ious teammate is probably not giving you enough in part because
you are not worth as much to him or her as you should be. In
fact, you are the best judge of why your teammate is withholding.

If you have a serious problem with a mate that loves you too
little to share the wealth and you have decided to struggle it out
(because that's exactly what it will be), you will have to devote
your attention to financial fact-gathering. It is only by getting your
fair share of the planning process and therefore the budgeting and
spending process that you will wrest for yourself your financial
due. It will not make your relationship any smoother, but it will
stop your money fights where they start, usually at the budgeting
issues. If you find that every time you prioritize, your spouse
insists that his priorities take precedence over yours, you are
going to have to make some hard decisions. In the chapter de-

voted to Conflict Resolution (chapter 6), I explain the importance of simply "taking turns" at getting what you want.

SEX ROLES AND FIGHTS

As you identify the role that you and your mate play in making financial decisions and handling money matters, you will most likely find that those roles depend largely on whether you are male or female. Our culture prescribes many roles, and they are still largely based on gender. We still believe that men are more financially astute, and should carry the major money-making and investing burden. Once I gave a talk in an affluent New Jersey community, and I joked that all men in the audience would probably love to have a husband. I never got so many affirmations from men in my life. No matter how unrealistic this superprovider image is, we carry it with us. We still believe that women should be more dependent and are less capable and more scattered when it comes to money matters. We believe this whether we are male or female. Financial discrimination exists, and anyone who believes that it doesn't has been living in a cave.

It could be the coquette in her or the macho man in him that creates the imbalance (most likely it's a little of both). Women are more likely to admit their ignorance, even flaunt it so they can be taken care of. Men are more likely to stonewall and cover their ignorance with a strong silence. This can leave both of them in the dark and neither of them making money as a team.

In the past two decades sex biases have changed, at least legally and politically, but have they changed culturally? It's your family culture that counts. What gender roles were taught to you? To find out, take Silent Survey #9.

Silent Survey #9

How good were your parents at keeping sex out of the boardroom?

What connections do you make between gender and money?

Who handled the money in your home, mother or father?

Who earned the money in your home, mother, father or both?

What did you overhear, if anything, about their money discussions? What disturbs you most about your memories?

Did you feel that there was a definite power imbalance between the two of them?

If your parents remarried, did you detect a difference in the new family? How did you react to the difference?

If you had a sibling of the opposite sex, were you treated differently from him or her when it came to money because of the difference in your gender?

Were you overtly taught that women are to be taken care of and men are to be the supporting spouse?

Once again you must look beyond your past family history to what you have become as an adult. Reflect on your responses to the following statements:

I do believe that men and women are equally capable of handling money.

I still feel that women should be taken care of even though I wish I didn't feel this way.

Women can do a lot when it comes to budgeting and cash flow, but important investment decisions have to be made by the breadwinner, whether it be the man or the woman.

This Silent Survey is particularly difficult for many of my clients. I've seen many a high-powered career woman forced to admit that she believes women should be taken care of financially. I've also heard many a modern "liberated" man confess that he feels men are superior in handling money. Conversely, many an Archie Bunker type secretly knows that Edith has a better grasp of the stock market than he does. It is imperative that you be as truthful as possible with yourself and with your mate when analyzing your associations between gender and money.

When this Silent Survey is taken honestly and shared, it sheds enormous light on the origin of your money fights. Remember the results of this survey as you begin to keep the fight diaries outlined in chapter 4. If you find that sexual role-play brings you into conflict, there are certain mechanical things you can do to stop fighting without going through years of therapy.

If one or both of you believe that the female teammate is less capable of handling money than the other, *reverse all money tasks for two weeks*. For example, have all budgeting and bill paying done by him and all tax and investment planning by her. Give each other instructions first (in the *boardroom,* of course). You both know full well that nothing drastic will happen. Tasks will be done differently, perhaps a little less efficiently at first, but decisions will be made and bills will be paid, and IRAs will be funded.

What if your mate won't go along with this? What if she gets the little-girl giggles or becomes resentful about budgeting and won't accept a more powerful role? What if he maintains that a woman's place is in the kitchen and won't give up his power over her?

That depends. Do either of you really *want* to change? If not, your attitudes, albeit old-fashioned, are at least "in sync" with each other's. If, however, the less powerful one (usually the wife) is unhappy, she's going to have to take a few chances. Last year I appeared on "Phil Donahue" to discuss women and money. At least one male caller and two female callers asserted that in their household the husband made all the financial decisions and handled all the money, even the wife's paycheck. The men believed that it wasn't the wife's job to handle money. Besides, they couldn't do it anyway, they said.

These wives are financially abused women. They need first to understand that power over money is power over the relationship, and thus something is very imbalanced within their marriage. Once the women are ready to assert themselves, surprising results occur. They make demands, they make suggestions, they make decisions, and they make a fuss! And they improve their lot in the marriage as a result.

When he meets with such rebellion, the husband who has withheld money and power can only do one of three things: he can rethink his position and begin to share; he can become more withholding and create more hostility; or he can leave the relationship.

If the husband decides to share, the situation is improved. It is rare that a husband will leave over this issue, although it is the secret fear of the financially abused wife. Such a catastrophic result is almost always associated with other marital problems, such as an extramarital affair. The most common result is the second, that the husband will become more withholding and create additional hostility. What to do?

Decide whether you want to solve the problem with or without couples counseling. It's easier with, but if you must act alone, do break out of old-fashioned role models and do the following.

Learn everything you can from books and seminars (keep quiet while learning, to avoid discouragement from your partner). Borrow money from friends, relatives, or your household and invest it, no matter how small the amount (try for $500–$1,500). Emerge with a demand for autonomy—your own checking account, credit card, or boardroom consultations.

If you change your role, your teammate must do so too, because otherwise there will be no one to play with! It has been suggested to me (by a man) that if a woman can "fake it in bed, she can fake it at the bank." He meant that if all else fails the wife can secretly squirrel away some household money without her husband's knowledge. But that adds the syndrome of secrecy to the syndrome of inequality. Ultimately, I don't suggest a secret hoard. Why? Because women should not be reduced to "pilfering" instead of investing. If your sexual role has debased you, you'll feel it. If your mate won't change, you must.

So much for the woman's burden. What about the man's? He's expected to work for the wife and kids, ask for nothing for himself except a little TV and an occasional night out. He's saddled with having to earn a salary, invest it, and be supremely knowledgable in a world of complex investment choices for which even a graduate education never prepared him. What's a guy to do? He probably wishes he had a husband! Add to this a wife whose idea of economy is buying one Gucci purse instead of two, and a kid with a bad case of the "gimmes," and you can see how a good husband can get an ulcer or heart attack. Statistically, they usually do!

Remember, men: Saints don't get married. You don't have to be perfect, to meet every need, to always put the family first. What's more, you don't have to know everything about money. You're allowed to rely on your wife 50 percent of the time. What if she resents it and expects you to take care of all the finances? You'll have to admit your needs to yourself and to her. Encourage her to help. Start slow, perhaps with budgeting or checkbook balances. Recommend books and courses for her to take. I've never met a woman who didn't ultimately respond to a man who showed her the respect to believe she could handle money.

In short, if either of you want to change your sex-based values, start with yourself first. Many of the exercises, particularly the task-oriented and joint decision-making steps are "gender neutral." Soon you will be, too.

II

IDENFIFYING YOUR FIGHT PATTERNS

The Fight Diary

4

YOU'VE probably already recognized yourself in some of the styles and patterns of fighting described in this book. We all share some of each. However, to really achieve more money and less turmoil in your own life, it's necessary for you to catalog your own fundamental fighting patterns. Using a diary will help you become more aware of how, when, and why you fight about money and to focus on the results of those fights. More often than not, money fights use up the energy you need for true financial planning.

Ask yourself right now: How and when do I fight? Do I accomplish anything by it? This last question may seem facetious, but many people find that fighting serves a purpose. For example, a fight can speed up a money decision. Yet, most people would prefer not to fight. If this sounds like you, remember that even though fights may seem useful at times, there are better ways of getting things done. Your fight pattern diary will help.

Aside from the timing, style, and end result of your fights, it's instructive to notice *where* your fights take place. Do they happen in the car, at your mother-in-law's house, on vacation? If so, you've taken your money matters out of the boardroom and brought them into the bedroom. Money matters can be aggravating. Discussing them "on the run," such as while driving to work in heavy traffic, is an inevitable death knell to good financial planning. It also produces a tension that increases the likelihood of fights.

KEEPING THE DIARY

To identify your fight pattern, use the diary system outlined in the box below. Keep your diary in a separate notebook used just for that purpose. Jot down the date, approximate time, and place each money fight occurs. Note the subject matter of the fight and the circumstances or incidents that immediately preceded the fight. Finally, describe the result of that fight. How did it end? What was its ultimate impact on your financial situation? Notice that I do not ask you to write down who won the fight; that's irrelevant to making money.

This diary must be taken seriously to be effective. The "recurring themes" of a marriage are found among money-fight patterns. Like drug addiction, the habit is very hard to change and can be fatal; according to Dr. Jürg Willi, author of *Couples in Collusion:*

> The neurotic game of collusion can be assumed to take over when both partners become caught up in a formalized fighting ritual which drains them of mental energy for long periods and thus prevents them either from reaching a solution or from escaping the trap. The battle itself may become the very substance of living for scores of years, as if the partners came to daggers and effectively tore their lives to shreds. Psychosomatic illnesses can develop under these conditions of contin-

FIGHT PATTERN DIARY

Date:

Time:

Place:

Incidents leading up to fight:

Subject matter of fight:

Ultimate effect on financial decision making:

Other comments:

ual stress and may prove fatal. It is difficult for an observer to understand how two people could become enraged over such childish tri-
fles. The partners often behave as if they were not quite sane; they
cannot tolerate rational discussion and lack the ability to see the relationship objectively. In all matters external to their relationship, however, they appear to be open, approachable, understanding and in
harmony with others.[3]

Before analyzing your diary pages, be sure you have an adequate number of examples. I find that a minimum of six diaried
fights or "heated discussions" is necessary before a true pattern of
fighting begins to emerge. Some people need a dozen. Few need
more.

At first, your fighting may appear to be random. Over time,
however, I guarantee you that a fight pattern that can be identified and eventually broken will become apparent. For some of
you, money fights are frequent, and it won't take long for you to
develop a diary with sufficient examples to begin work. For others, there are long periods between fights. If you want to get
going fast, think back to the last couple of fights you had and try
to recreate them mentally for the diary. Don't precipitate a money
fight just to get to work on this project (yes, I have known people
who have done so).

Once you have your adequate sample to work from, don't stop
there. For people with severe money fight problems, maintaining
the diary (perhaps all their lives) can be therapeutic. It helps di-
minish the intensity of the fights because it shows clearly what's
really going on. In fact, the diary tells the story of what underlies
the money fights.

Alfred Hitchcock used the word "McGuffin" to indicate that the
plot of a story was only a vehicle for what was really happening,
a good suspense technique. Often money fights are only a
"McGuffin," a substitute for what the couple really wants to fight
about, but fears they cannot resolve. As you describe the fight in
your diary, determine whether the topic of the fight was really a
smokescreen for something else that you wanted to deal with,

something different that you really wanted to say. The faster you bring out the true basis of your problem, the faster you can get on with making money.

Each of you should prepare your own separate diary. There's too much counterinfluence if you jot down your thoughts on the fights together. You are better off with two inaccurate accounts than one inaccurate account, because with two accounts you can see how each partner's experience differs from the other's. You should make your analyses separately as well; this way, it is not necessary for either of you to read the other's diary. In the beginning you may wish to keep the diaries private so that you don't rehash the fight a second time, wasting time and energy.

HOW TO ANALYZE THE FIGHTS

Once you have acknowledged the existence of the money fights and have determined their usual time, place, and topic, you are ready to analyze the fights so that you can do something about them. Remember, your purpose is either (1) to stop fighting about money; (2) to avoid money fights; or (3) to tolerate money fights because they actually enhance your financial situation.

Naturally, the first goal is the hardest to attain. To stop fighting, you'll probably have to know the purpose of the fight and solve your underlying emotional problems. Avoiding the fight is much easier. All that is required of you is that you either avoid the situation that precipitates the fight, avoid the topic, or do your money planning strictly in the boardroom. For those of you who find that money making is possible despite the fights, you may wish to tolerate a certain amount of money fighting and keep the decision-making process separate.

To approach these goals, analyze your money fights with respect to the following six aspects:

Frequency
Length

Mode
Recurring circumstances or theme
Simplified character analysis
Base problem

Frequency and *length* are the two variables that are easiest to discern. The longer and more frequent the fighting, the more severe your problem and the more important it will be to work on stopping your fights rather than merely avoiding them. It is difficult to pin down an "average" or "normal" frequency and length for money fights, but from my many years counseling couples it seems the average is quite high, with a money-related fight occurring a minimum of once every week and lasting about twenty minutes. The more important question is whether the frequency and length of your money fights troubles you. If so, they must be analyzed further.

Your *mode* of fighting as well tells a great deal about whether you are getting somewhere financially or whether the fight itself is preventing you from making money together. Try to categorize each fight according to one of the following modes.

On-point money fights are fights that are specifically about money and occur when money topics are brought up by the couple or one partner. Usually these fights involve a clash of priorities. For example, Mrs. Jones wants to buy a new coat, so she brings up the subject with her husband. He thinks they can't afford it. She feels deprived and hasn't had a good coat in a long time. They fight over their budget and ability to spend. This is an on-point money fight. The issue is money, the disagreement is in regard to money, and the solution will be a financial-planning one.

Off-point money fights are fights that involve money even though nothing actually has to be done or decided with respect to money issues. For example, the couple is having a fight over his coming home late from the office. He claims he works hard and that his career will suffer if he doesn't stay late. She mutters something about his having nothing to show financially for his labors. They fight over money. This is an off-point money fight, because money becomes the subject matter of the fight even though nothing specific toward the couple's financial planning has to be achieved. These fights are usually the result of disappointments in the marriage and dashed financial expectations. The best remedy for them is avoidance by pledging to talk about money only in the boardroom atmosphere. As a temporary alternative, the fights can be suffered through as long as financial planning schedules for boardroom meetings are religiously adhered to and financial planning takes place despite the occurrence of the fights.

Subject-specific money fights involve a recurring theme. They may be on point or off point; that is, they may crop up where money actually is at issue, or at any old time and on any occasion. They are distinguished by the same old complaint, usually about past investment mistakes, low income, or overspending, being rehashed *ad nauseum*. For example, every time the conversation turns to money, somehow it subtly builds to a fight over the fact that she hasn't had a vacation in three years and that it's depriving her family. She then points out that the husband lost $5,000 in a speculative investment three years ago. This mistake crops up in every money conversation and even during fights regarding non-money-oriented topics.

This couple's fighting displays two recurring themes, one off point, the other on point. The on-point theme (occurring only when money matters are discussed) is the wife's vacation. She is resentful, perhaps about working in general, and so any attempts at budgeting degenerate into a tirade surrounding her vacation needs.

Simultaneously, the husband's past investment mistake is a constant source of irritation to the wife, a symbol of why she must work and be deprived of a vacation. This complaint is addressed both during discussions of money and on other "off point" occasions. For example, he says, "The house hasn't been very clean lately." She retorts, "Well, if you hadn't lost all that money on that crummy investment, maybe we would have a maid." She never expresses her anger at his taking no responsibility for housecleaning, even though they both work. Such a fixation on a recurring theme usually means that there has been a disappointment regarding money expectations. Harping on the theme prevents the couple from dealing with present problems and creates a time warp in which old wounds are opened and new matters are left unattended. The problem should be isolated and treated separately, keeping money matters in the boardroom.

Planning-avoidance fights take place when money matters are at issue but where the subject matter of the fight is not money at all. For example, Jane and Joe must do their taxes. Money is very much at issue, but they don't fight over it. Instead, she begins to chat about their daughter's teacher and how she believes that the teacher is not responsive enough to the child's needs. He counters that the school knows what it's doing and she shouldn't be so doting on the daughter's every whim. She accuses him of calling her a bad mother, and they fight over the relationship between mother and daughter. Money issues are never addressed. This mode of fighting usually stems from a desire to avoid the money issue at hand (paying taxes) or the need for a useful pattern of communication regarding money. It is the easiest to solve because eventually the boardroom setting will force new money habits.

The diaries will show immediately whether your fights have a *recurring circumstance* or a *recurring theme*. For example, if you always fight right before sex, you've got your recurring circumstance. A visit to a well-to-do sibling or a vacation trip are two circumstances that often precipitate recurring fights. Your diaries will highlight these themes and circumstances.

It may interest you to compare your themes to those revealed in a survey conducted by *Working Woman* magazine in 1985:

Husband's overspending—10 percent of all fights
Priorities—33 percent of all fights
A feeling of too little money—33 percent of all fights
Wife's overspending—24 percent of all fights

FIGHTING MODES

Type	Description	Usual Cause
On point	Money is the issue; subject matter of fight is money	Failure to plan, failure to communicate, feelings of inequality in the relationship, different priorities
Off point	Money is not the real issue; subject matter of fight is money	Disappointment or dashed expectations in money matters
Subject specific	Money may or may not be the issue; fight is always about same money habit or past incident	Dashed expectations, different priorities
Planning avoidance	Money is the issue; subject matter of fight is not money	Failure to communicate

In the next chapter you will become familiar with a variety of money syndromes in which each member of the couple plays a specific role. They are, of necessity, simplified so that each role becomes a prototype. In order to identify which money syndrome best fits your own fight pattern, you need to do a *simplified character analysis* for yourself and your mate. For those of you who are working together and comparing your diary analyses, this can be a most important step.

For example, Joe is always yelling at Jane because she can't balance her checkbook. They never sit down and balance it together, and he never does the work for her. Instead, he just stomps around the room screaming at her for her irresponsibility. Jane usually ends up crying, hurt and angry at the same time. She eventually does a tearful reconciliation of the checkbook while he loudly proclaims that he is going to tear up her charge cards. A quick character analysis here would show a Doll's House Syndrome, with the husband holding the purse strings tightly in his fist. As you become familiar with the various syndromes (they're listed in chapter 4), you might want to characterize your fights regularly so you can see which areas of financial planning will be the hardest for you in light of the syndrome you exhibit.

Finally, you will be able to identify what I call the *base problem*. In chapter 4, you will learn that all syndromes develop because of one of four base problems in the money relationship: Inequality, Conflicting Priorities, Dashed Expectations, and Failure to Communicate. Knowing which ones burden you can prepare you to work together despite the problem.

Inequality.   Fights resulting from actual or perceived inequality.

Conflicting Priorities.   Fights resulting from differences in goals, tastes, and priorities.

Dashed Expectations.   Fights resulting from financial disappointments or envy of family and friends.

Failure to Communicate.   Fights resulting because the couple doesn't know how to talk about money.

After you have each completed your diary analysis, you should sit down together and compare notes. Do you agree on the frequency of your fights and their circumstances? One of you may consider certain discussions as fighting and the other one may not even have jotted down the incident. Do you agree on the mode of fighting? If you do, you'll have a much better chance of keeping money matters in the boardroom. If you have agreed that there is a recurring theme to your fights, you have a good chance of making that topic taboo when real money issues come up. If you agree that money fights are only a substitute for other problems, then you know that you have a serious unrelated problem that you should isolate and deal with. If you can agree on which role you play, you can go immediately to the syndromes listed on page 78 and try to recognize yourself. In the meantime, let's take a look at two couples' sample diaries and practice by analyzing their cases.

Millie and Paul

Millie is a computer programmer making $35,000 a year. Paul is a journalist making $18,000 a year and planning to work his way up to media broadcasting. They are both thirty-four years old; they are childless and have been married for eight years. Although their combined income is over $50,000 a year, they never seem to be able to make ends meet. They have no financial program, and they will tell you that they fight over money constantly. When asked about the nature of their fights, they both say, "we fight over everything, but mostly about not having enough money." They have no further insights except that Paul believes Millie spends a little too much money and she believes Paul makes much too little money. They've been nervous about their finances since they reached the age of thirty since they'd like to start having children soon.

Date: November 26, 1986
Time: 10:00 A.M.
Place: The couple's car while driving to Paul's mother's house for Thanksgiving dinner.
Incidents leading up to fight: Paul mentioned that he'd like to take a vacation in January. He wanted to go someplace quiet where he could work on a short story he would like to try to have published. Millie said there wasn't enough money for a vacation. They could hardly pay their American Express bill.
Subject matter of fight: She berated him for not making enough money to "make ends meet" (a recurring theme in their arguments). She also said that she wanted to go someplace where there

69

was sightseeing and not just lie around on some beach being lazy and nonproductive.

Ultimate effect on financial planning: They decided to take a package trip to England in January, charge it on their credit card, and pay for the trip somehow in February.

Date: Christmas Week, 1986 (dinnertime)
Place: The living room of the couple's studio apartment
Incidents leading up to fight: Seemingly nothing—Paul came home from the office late and Millie lit into him.
Subject matter of fight: She insisted that he quit his job and get a new one.
Ultimate effect on financial planing: None. He absolutely refused to change his career path and declared that she could leave him if she wanted to make that choice.
Other comments: On the day of the fight, Millie had received a $5,000 special end-of-year bonus and had used it to pay the American Express bill.

Date: January 4, 1987 (midnight)
Place: Russell Square Hotel, London
Incidents leading up to fight: Millie purchased and shipped home a large set of expensive dishes and purchased a good many English tailored skirts.
Subject matter of fight: Her overspending
Ultimate effect on financial planning: None. She told Paul her spending was none of his business and she didn't want to hear another word about it. If he didn't like it, he could choose to leave her.

As a trained advisor, I know exactly what these people should be doing and what is bothering them. But my knowing it, and even my telling them about it, won't help them half as much as their understanding their own problems through self-analysis. Let's take a look at their diaries and see how they should proceed to stop fighting about money and make some.

Although the sample is skimpy, let's consider it as representative and work from the three instances. Pay attention to frequency, length, mode, recurring circumstances or theme, base problem, and simplified character analysis.

First you will see that the fights are rather frequent, with at least three blowups in a six-week period. Consequently, the fighting is interfering with their ability to accomplish any serious financial planning. Note that the places of these fights and the times differ in each case. There is no recurring location or circumstances that triggers the fight. This makes things harder for the couple; merely avoiding their mother-in-law's house, or not talking about money in the car, will not solve their problem.

It's interesting to analyze their fighting modes. As a rereading will show, they are on-point fighters. Notice that on Thanksgiving they are fighting over money, and the subject of the fight is money. The issue is how much to spend on a vacation and whether they can afford one in the first place. Around Christmas, they're fighting because Millie spent her entire bonus without getting any reward for herself. At first blush, it may not appear that this is the cause of the fight, since Millie merely hauled off at her husband as soon as he walked in the door. But remember that she received $5,000 as a bonus, and she punished herself by granting herself no reward when she received the extra money. Instead of being joyful, she reinforced her feeling that she was the only breadwinner and was not being properly taken care of by her husband. The third fight was also on point; the problem was budgeting. He thought she was overspending. She was angry because now, when she finally received her reward, he had the temerity to question and berate her.

There is an underlying and recurring theme that runs through these three fights. Neither party feels secure about their spending habits, both believe they are in financial trouble, and yet they don't have any organized budget or cash flow procedure. When they want something, like a skirt or a vacation, they fight over whether it's affordable. When they receive money (like a bonus), they pay the first bill they have and lose control over the money immediately.

Let's look at the base problems in Millie and Paul's case. Millie is angry that Paul has a job that does not bring as much immediate income as hers does. The base problem is Inequality. The wife is earning more than the husband, and she resents him for it. The husband, in turn, hates her resentment. He feels that he too is contributing to the marriage and is on an important career path. He wants to have as much say about family finances as does his wife, even if what he has to say is to criticize her spending.

Despite their problems, neither ever threatens to leave the other, although each has invited the other to leave. *This is a sign that they will probably stay together,* since neither actually took the initiative to leave. Yet to stay together they must improve their financial picture. They don't communicate well about money, they don't make decisions together, and worst of all they don't divide tasks or work from a known data base. Instead they make gratuitous comments ("We can't afford a vacation. We have to pay the American Express bill"). They work in a car or any old place. They must learn to take their money matters out of the bedroom and into the boardroom.

Sarah and Terry

Sarah is a fifty-year-old New York City school teacher who has been entitled to receive her pension since she was forty-three, having put twenty years in the system. Terry is a fifty-five-year-old midlevel corporate executive who could take retirement next year if he chose. Their two children are grown and gone; their grandchildren are the apples of their eye. One of their children is divorced, and they feel obliged to provide gifts in one way or another for the grandchildren of about $8,000 a year. During their thirty years of marriage they have not fought unduly about money. They both worked, they both supported the home, they both assumed traditional sex roles proudly and without disturbance. They seem even to have gotten through their forties without a midlife crisis. So how come they are fighting about money all the time now? These excerpts from their diary may give you some clues.

Date: January 6, 1986
Place: A room in an expensive hotel in Puerto Rico
Events leading up to the fight: Terry lost $1,000 gambling at the casino. His wife is furious.
Subject matter of fight: Sarah dumps out two shopping bags full of souvenirs and says that she is planning to return everything because Terry is leading them into the poorhouse with his irresponsibility. He feels ashamed and defensive about losing the money. He counters by saying that it never happened to him before and that they could afford it.
Ultimate effect on financial planning: None. The rest of the vacation is strained but cordial.

Date: March 15, 1986
Place: The office of the couple's accountant
Events leading up to the fight: The accountant has suggested that Terry put more money into his corporate pension plan. The accountant is not sure what the 1989 tax law will bring, and he'd like Terry to "sock away" as much money for his retirement as he possibly can.
Subject matter of fight: Sarah thinks this is a great idea and wants to make a budget to see how much they could afford to maximize his pension contribution. Terry says no, and surprises both his accountant, an old friend, and Sarah by announcing that he's planning to buy a boat. His wife mutters, "Over my dead body." The accountant is a little uncomfortable and suggests that he look over their tax documents and that they meet again. The fight continues on the way home, with Sarah dumbfounded over this new suggestion and Terry furious over the fact that he doesn't seem to be getting anything "for his years of hard work."
Ultimate effect on financial planning: They decide to postpone the decision about the boat until the spring and try to obtain some advance news about post-Reagan tax act changes.

Date: August 1986

Place: The couple's living room

Events leading up to fight: Terry has just told his wife that he has made a loan to his brother-in-law of $40,000.

Subject matter of fight: Sarah is hysterical. She can't believe he's done such a thing, particularly without consulting her. He's never behaved this way before. She's terrified that they are going to lose part of their nest egg. "Don't worry," says Terry. "We have plenty of time to make it up, and besides, he'll pay it back." She becomes a little bit calmer and says to him, "Terry, I am absolutely planning to retire and I want you to retire as well."

Ultimate effect on financial planning: The couple came for long-term retirement planning.

For many men and women it is very difficult to face the concept of retirement. They may even dip into well-planned retirement funds just to keep themselves working. Many people make the worst mistakes in their financial lives to avoid retirement. I know executives who have lost their jobs or taken risks that they have never taken before just when retirement becomes possible. On the other hand, for others, like Sarah, retirement is something they can hardly wait for. This is particularly true for civil servants, who usually think of retirement as the greatest benefit of their jobs.

Sarah and Terry's money fighting was a symptom of the breakdown of the successful attitudinal structure that had bound them together for years. Terry began to make important financial decisions (gambling, lending money, buying luxuries) alone, without Sarah's participation. He was certain Sarah would condemn his new lifestyle, since he knew she wanted them both to retire. Instead, he subconsciously intended to lose, spend, or give away enough money to make that impossible. Because of his lack of trust, she felt a frightening loss of the autonomy she had always enjoyed. Ultimately, they would have lost all sense of prosperity and teamwork.

However, they were able to salvage the situation by seeking

help. When they came to my office it was clear that neither frequency, length, mode, nor recurring theme was of critical importance in their arguments. They had fought only a few times over major decisions. It was important, though, to take a careful look at the content of their fights to get at their base problem.

During the first session it became evident to them that for the first time in their relationship they were suffering from Conflicting Priorities. His goal was to keep on working; her goal was to retire. After extensive financial planning, they did both. The couple purchased a lake house (with a boat slip). Sarah would rather have traveled around the world, but Terry continued to work four days a week, slowing down more than he wished, but nevertheless remaining very active in business. The couple began a long-term retirement plan. The result was a compromise that put the two back in financial control by allowing both the excitement of a work life and the relaxation of a country home.

After you've thoroughly analyzed your own fight patterns, it's time to see how they fit into the various fight syndromes that I have identified in the couples I have counseled. Categorizing syndromes is not in and of itself helpful to a couple. But I have found that after they've done their own personal analysis, it is useful for couples to compare their patterns or problems to those of other couples, and then apply the techniques that have worked in these situations. We'll now examine the most common money syndromes for couples today.

5

The 25 Most Common Money Syndromes

In my seventeen years of counseling couples in financial planning, I have encountered twenty-five money syndromes that fall roughly into the four base problems identified in the last chapter. These are fairly easy to label and remember, since they come from patterns of behavior found in literature, movies, television, and wherever else character analyses are drawn. If you respond to the label, the syndrome may very well apply to you and your mate.

Note once more your reaction to the base problems of Inequality, Conflicting Priorities, Dashed Expectations, and Failure to Communicate as they are defined back on page 68. You'll see they have nothing to do with the actual wealth or debt of a couple, but instead summarize how couples interact when it comes to money matters.

Inequality

The Doll's House Syndrome. He handles all the money; she is treated like a child.

The Breadwinner Syndrome. He makes most of the money and all the decisions.

The Lolita Syndrome. She gets indulged for every whim, he is a beast of burden.

The Princess in the New World Syndrome. She makes most of the money and all the decisions, and she is angry with him for his low income.

The Beer and Bread Syndrome. He works and takes money for his entertainment and leaves her to manage the household on the rest.

The Ralph Kramden Syndrome. He takes or makes too little and is broke before the end of the week.

The Daddy Warbucks Syndrome. One of them gets money from a rich parent.

Conflicting Priorities

The Now vs. Later Syndrome. One wants immediate gratification, the other wants to save for the future.

The Tangible vs. Intangible Syndrome. One wants a new house, the other wants a vacation.

The Kids vs. Us Syndrome. One puts the couple first, the other the kids.

The Sunshine vs. Wall Street Syndrome. One doesn't care about money, the other is very, very interested.

The Oscar Wilde Syndrome. He says, "Give me the luxuries of life and I'll dispense with the necessities." She says, "Are you kidding?"

The Peter Pan Syndrome. He never wants to retire, she's ready to travel.

Dashed Expectations

The Disappointed Woman, Part I. He doesn't earn enough, he's not smart enough about money, they don't have enough.

The Disappointed Woman, Part II. Same as above but she earns enough and they do have enough, but it doesn't come from him, so it's not good.

The Disappointed Man, Part I. He doesn't earn enough and somehow it's her fault.

The Disappointed Man, Part II. She wants, wants, wants—all she does is demand.

The Inflation Babies. How come they don't have as much as their parents? Why are prices so high? Are they becoming downwardly mobile?

The Second Marriage Shifty Eye. Expectations were dashed the first time around, how will it work out this time?

The Duke of Windsor Syndrome. They are disappointed in not receiving an expected inheritance.

Failure to Communicate

The Rumpelstiltskin Syndrome. He's secretive about money, she can only guess about his assets.

The Poor Little Lamb Syndrome. She's totally ignorant, can't even balance a checkbook, and doesn't want to hear a thing about finances.

The I've Got a Secret Syndrome. One is hiding debts or problems.

The Sexual Tension Syndrome. They fight about money to avoid sex.

Now go back and review the list. Do you recognize yourself, your aunt Sadie, your cousin Marvin? These are all characterizations of how people transact their personal financial business with their mates.

Now let's examine each of these syndromes to see how they actually work in the couple's financial and personal lives.

INEQUALITY

It is very difficult to discuss the Inequality base problem without being sexist! This problem is not "gender neutral"; Inequality falls more on women than on men. Furthermore, women and men treat unequal earning power differently. Historically we are quite used to the Doll's House Syndrome, where daddy-husband brings home the bacon and the childlike wife pretends to be too scattered to handle the funds. Things went along smoothly this way for at least the past fifty years. But recently a lot of women have been getting angry. Fights are raging around too much autonomy on the part of the breadwinner-husband. Things get even worse when the husband is not making more or appreciably more than the wife, and he *still* expects to control the purse strings.

Oddly enough, the situation is not parallel when the woman is the breadwinner and controls the purse strings. Frequently she is just as resentful, if not more so, at the helplessness of the husband. After all, he was supposed to be the hunter, she the gatherer. Even when the husband acknowledges his financial inferiority and gives the wife the purse strings to hold, she often takes it resentfully, instead of with the sangfroid that the husband displayed when he controlled the funds. Indeed, the Princess in the New World is very likely to earn the money, make the decisions, and not like it one bit.

By contrast, Lolita expects to be supported in fine style. Money is for her husband to worry over. Yet Lolita has no intention of making any contribution to the relationship. Basically, she is exchanging her companionship for his financial support. This may work for a time. But eventually the couple fights over her spending.

In the Beer and Bread Syndrome the husband is the provider and king. But what he does with his money is rather peculiar. He brings home his paycheck to his wife and gives himself a reward off the top. She's left to manage the household with the rest, no matter what. He pays himself first, so to speak, and then berates her if she cannot manage. But sometimes the poor man makes a mistake. This happens in the Ralph Kramden Syndrome, when he's not quite generous enough to himself and runs out of money before the end of the week. This leaves him begging to his wife-mother for a few extra dollars so he can go bowling. He's created an upper-hand situation but handed her the superior position because of his own bad management.

The only blameless Inequality syndrome (Daddy Warbucks) occurs when one party is just plain richer than the other from a source outside the couple's efforts. This happens because of an inheritance, a settlement of an insurance or court claim (I have known many of these), or a former marriage settlement. In such cases financial autonomy has gone just too far and one party feels upset.

If there is great disparity, the possibility of differences in lifestyle between the partners come up. Should they live according to their individual means, or should they live according to the means of the couple? Unless they both have access to the other's money, there is a sense of profound unfairness. He certainly is not going to be able to go on a ski trip and leave her home without being considered a cheapskate and a heel.

The Union Man

Ida and Jack have been married for twelve years, and both feel they are doing pretty well financially. He has a skilled job and delights in letting people know he's a "union man" with a nicely negotiated benefits package. Ida did not work for the first eight years of their marriage. But now she's a secretary and earns about 50 percent of what Jack earns. She has no benefits other than the salary.

The couple's financial planning procedure was set early in their marriage and hasn't changed one bit, even though they have. Jack was always the breadwinner, and there was a general consensus that he would be making the major decisions concerning where they would live, how much they would contribute to the employee savings plan, and the type of vacation they would have. Of course, Ida had a say in many of these things, particularly when it involved the home. But this was because Jack didn't really mind, not because he felt she was more powerful or even equal as a decision maker.

Although Jack was a "good provider," Ida always had a vague feeling that she was not protected. She secretly dreaded their future and felt she would be left with nothing if the marriage ever broke up. Ida looked forward to the day when the kids would be old enough for her to start working.

For the first three years of their marriage Ida and Jack had no money fights. In fact, they never spoke about money at all, since Ida accepted her role gladly. She was only twenty-one when they married; Jack was twenty-six, and she looked at him as older and wiser. Also, she was busy with two young children.

This might have gone on for some years except for an event that had absolutely nothing to do with money (sort of). Jack had an affair and Ida found out (actually, he confessed it to her in the fourth year of their marriage). Ida was naturally hurt, angry, and confused. She decided to stay in the marriage, but one thing never left her mind. Jack had taken a rather lavish vacation with the other woman and had bought her some gifts, including a ring. In the four years of their marriage, Ida had never received any treats of this nature. In fact, she had been frugal with the household money he gave her every week. While the marriage continued after the affair, the peacefulness regarding money did not. There seemed to be a fight at least once a week.

Ida usually started the fight on a Friday night after both had had a long, hard week. Usually she complained about his not having enough insurance, her not being able to pay the bills, the house being too small, or some other attack on his ability to provide. Jack's defense was not to communicate. He read his paper, left the house, or watched TV. In the fifth year of their marriage, Ida began to skim some of the money she was getting from him every week and put it in a money market account under her own name. She believed Jack knew nothing about this. She was wrong. He suspected from the beginning and once or twice even actually gave her some extra money for household use so she'd have more to "steal." Jack would occasionally feel guilty about his affair and considered this part of his penance. Nevertheless, he never overtly gave her any extra money or acceded to her demands to share more of his paycheck with the family. Meanwhile, Jack was using the money he had withheld for himself. At the end of a week he couldn't imagine where it had all gone. Ida thought he was secretly saving it or maybe spending it on a woman. Neither was true.

When Ida was thirty and their youngest child turned eight, Ida got a job with a fair salary and steady hours, but no benefits. Ida was ecstatic; she expected everything about their finances to change. After all, Jack was thirty-five years old and had held the same job for fifteen years. With her new salary, they were really going to "get ahead."

But in fact the couple's money fights became more frequent. Except now it seemed that the initiator of the fights was Jack. He would complain that her job was costing extra taxes, imploring her to quit because it was costing more money than it was worth. Or she would be late coming home (usually because of household shopping in the evening) and he would scream that her boss was taking advantage of her.

From the beginning, Ida had resolved not to give her paycheck to Jack. It was OK for him to be the provider, but she didn't have to be. She opened up her own money market account and used the money for extra things for herself. She thought of herself as doing quite well as some of the "extra money" was piling up.

She also had an unspoken belief that that money was all hers. It was her husband's responsibility to pay the taxes on all their funds. She also had a vague feeling that she should be doing something better with her money than leaving it in the money market fund, but she had no idea what the right thing to do was.

Meanwhile, Jack had no idea what his wife was doing with her money. To make himself feel more in control, he fantasized that she was putting it away for the children's education. Yet they never actually spoke about the children's education. She didn't want to bring it up because she didn't know how to deal with the enormity of the cost. He didn't want to bring it up because he was afraid he'd find that she wasn't saving for them after all.

Meanwhile, the economic world was changing all around them, and so were their friends. Every day they would hear radio and television commercials for new economic products. They had just recovered from the inflation of the 70s and had discovered money market funds. All of a sudden words like *no load mutual funds, unit trusts,* and *triple tax free bonds* were being tossed around. The last straw for Ida came when her hairdresser, elated, told her he had purchased 500 shares of Reebok stock and had sold them at an unheard-of price. Everybody was in the market, and she was left way behind.

What was worse, much worse, was that except for their own two-family house (they rented the second apartment at a below-market rate to a nice tenant who didn't bother them), they were *not in real estate.* Even Jack's apprentice owned two studio condominiums from which he derived income, and which were appreciating rapidly. Jack found the conversations at his favorite bar less about women and more about capital gains tax as the years went on. Everybody was looking for real estate, selling it, buying it, and trying to invest in some way or another. What was wrong with them? It must be that Ida never shared her money. That was it.

And then something bad happened to Jack. He lost his feeling of prosperity. He wasn't proud any more that he was a union man, nor did his benefits make him feel so secure. There was talk that there would be no Social Security. His wife was hiding all her money. He wasn't sure that his kids would get to college. He never seemed to have anything to say at the high-finance conversations at the local bar.

And that is when they came to see me. Trust, fair dealing, autonomy, and prosperity: these people were at the low end of the successful attitudinal scale, but they were by no means hopeless. They were both acting in concert, doing a fairly predictable economic dance, and combining the symptoms of several fight-pattern syndromes.

Certainly he was displaying the Breadwinner Syndrome. He earned the most money, thus he was going to dictate the terms of their finances. Her role was to follow his lead. Unfortunately, he had fallen into the Ralph Kramden Syndrome, where he really had too little money for himself. Actually Jack is a very family-conscious man, priding himself on being a "good provider." He never really wanted to deprive Ida or his kids. The result was that he took just enough for himself, and as inflation hit he found himself always a little short.

At first Ida played her role in the Breadwinner Syndrome. After she began to feel frustrated and insecure, she tried a little of the Lolita act. But being a hard-working and basically an honest woman, she decided to get a job and make her own money. This switched the actual earning capacity of the parties and created a new imbalance.

Their problem was still Inequality, but now the Inequality was not as black-and-white as it had been when only Jack worked. The result for Jack was a feeling of discomfort, even despondency, and eventually a feeling that he was not prospering. He had lost his role as sole provider.

But because there was a lack of health in their financial-planning relationship, the extra money did not bring the expected freedom. Instead, it fed into Ida's tendency to be noncommunicative, to be secretive about her money. She already had a tendency to squirrel away extra funds to make herself feel independent. Now she was clutching her hard-earned money to herself and not mingling it with the family funds. The worst part about this from a financial point of view is that she had no idea what to do with that money. It was accumulating, but it was not growing. In fact, she was so secretive about it she was afraid even to expose the amount she had.

Luckily, there were many positive things about the relationship between Ida and Jack. They didn't suffer from any of the Dashed Expectations syndromes. In fact, they had felt prosperous during most of the course of their marriage. It was only recently, when their friends were pulling ahead of them, that they lost that feeling, and it was in fact that loss that motivated them to take action. While their communication was spotty, neither of them was a liar. Perhaps most important, their priorities were the same. They wanted a family-oriented life together, and they wanted their money to serve that end. Nor did their Inequality ever escalate to the Doll's House type, where Ida was totally subservient and constantly victimized. Yes, there was a lot of hope for this couple.

But they were a disaster with respect to their *financial procedures*. In fact, they didn't practice any! The first step was to take their money matters out of the bedroom and into the boardroom. They had to reserve one hour a week every Thursday and resolve that at their own kitchen table (with the kids being taken care of by Grandma) they would work on their finances.

Within four months they had completed a graded net worth and liability statement and had repositioned their assets. Undoubtedly, they have stopped fighting about money and made some. But in their case much more was accomplished. They were able to escape their Inequality syndromes. Here's how it happened.

Because they both agreed to full disclosure in order to do joint data-gathering, both got some surprises. Jack found out how much money his wife had actually saved. It was much more than he thought. He also learned, as he feared, that she had no intention of providing for the children's education herself. She had had enough of self-sacrifice.

The real surprise, however, was for Ida. Ida found out that her husband did not have separate funds. This was at first a happy surprise, and then she got scared. He really was, in her mind, a lousy money manager. He finally acknowledged that she had done the little financial planning in which the couple had engaged, i.e., household management and bill paying. When it came to task division it turned out that Jack had a great tolerance for figures, calculations, and gathering data. Ida, working all day in her office, had the time and the atmosphere (and a handy phone for one or two personal calls) to keep in touch with a broker, read financial reports, and browse *The Wall Street Journal*. They both believed real estate would be a solid investment for them.

Another surprise for Ida was how well protected she would be in the event of Jack's death. Through his union, he had a pension that alleviated many of Ida's unrealistic fears about being a bag lady in her old age (a fear that many women at every economic level seem to share).

Once Ida learned how well she would be taken care of if Jack died, and even under the new divorce laws in the event they split up, she was able to be more aggressive with her investments. She started by placing $2,000 a year in an IRA, after I impressed on her the importance of long-term planning and the value of tax-deferred saving vehicles.

Ida continued to deposit her paychecks in her own separate money market account and disburse it, with Jack's knowledge, as she chose. It was acknowledged that while she would discuss her finances with Jack (mostly because she wanted to and they were both planning together so well), the money was hers.

Jack, on the other hand, continued to be the provider. He continued to take the money that he felt he needed (this time more realistically) and hand over the rest to Ida for use in the household. This time, however, he saw her more as a great asset to him, since she took the burden of paying bills off his shoulders. He also had an unspoken appreciation of the fact that she put the real estate they bought with her savings in both their names. They unquestionably became a team.

We're still working on college planning for the kids. Since their plan is new, we are waiting to see how the new tax law ultimately affects college planning. But I have no doubt that they will get around to it, together.

CONFLICTING PRIORITIES

The base problem of Conflicting Priorities is the easiest to handle through good money management. Fights over priorities occur when people just don't think the same way about money, such as in the Now vs. Later Syndrome. Some are interested in immediate gratification, such as a vacation, a new couch, a VCR. It's never time to plan for retirement, open an investment account, or concern themselves with their kids' education. The person looking to the future is usually considered a prig, a killjoy, and uptight. The other one may be called lazy, irresponsible, and a spendthrift. Related to the Now vs. Later Syndrome is the Tangible vs. Intangible Syndrome. These couples both want to spend money now, but they are interested in spending it on different things. One partner sees a car or a boat as something solid, a true investment, whereas a vacation or a good dinner out is wasteful. The other, of course, disagrees.

Closely related to the Tangible vs. Intangible Syndrome is the Oscar Wilde Syndrome—"Give me the luxuries in life and I'll dispense with the necessities." It's unimportant that there be a bank account balance or life insurance policy, so long as caviar is on the Friday night menu. Often this makes the other partner feel afraid and insecure.

The problem of Conflicting Priorities is very common in second marriages where new priorities must be set and old ones surrendered. Statistically, a previously married man is more likely to be living with or remarried to a never-married woman. Therefore, the woman is likely to have less joint decision-making experience, and the man is likely to feel more concerned about the power over his finances that he has surrendered by marrying again. This is particularly true if he has had a hard time in his first marriage.

In other priority problems, the kids are the issue at hand. This is particularly true of young couples adjusting to having a first child or in second marriages, in which the views about raising kids are different from those of the first marriage. Kids can be expensive, and when one parent gives greater financial priority to the needs of the children than to those of the other spouse, a fight is easy to start. Finally, there's the couple who does not handle well the differences in their views of the importance of money in general: the Sunshine vs. Wall Street Syndrome.

The Golden Couple

The "golden couple" were not originally my clients. I had seen them once or twice in our reception area waiting for one of our attorneys, who was handling their first real estate closing. They were about to buy a house in a suburb of Long Island. Their plan was to commute each day to their respective jobs in Manhattan. It was impossible to avoid noticing them. Charlie was simply gorgeous: thirty-three years old, tall, dark, and handsome. Charlene was no slouch either. She was about an inch taller than Charles, with Amy Irving hair and green eyes. They were a true golden couple, and a modern one at that.

Married for five years, no children (yet), they both had equally fast-track jobs at two different corporate headquarters. He was a biochemist whose only concern was that his company might move to an industrial park in New Jersey, and she was an up-and-coming account executive at a Madison Avenue advertising agency. What a nice future I could foresee for them!

The couple came to see me because they were about to buy their first home and wanted to make a new financial plan to accommodate the purchase. The conversation started innocently enough with the usual questions regarding their assets. Combined income (roughly equally earned) of $105,000 a year, fully taxable. No assets to speak of other than an $8,000 IRA held in a high-tech mutual fund. Each had $100,000 of life insurance provided by their employers. They both had a profit-sharing plan and had a vague knowledge of their pensions (we agreed we must all look into this). They had a total savings of $75,000 presently residing in a money market fund. Most of this ($50,000) was to be used for a down payment and closing costs on their new $262,000 home. The rest was money that Charlie said he was leaving in the account so that Charlene could decorate the house.

I began to talk about the wealth-building years of the couple, their short- and long-term goals, and the possibility that their pensions would not meet the lifestyle that they had become used to. I started to do a quick cash-flow chart and budget just to see their spending habits and figured that the situation required more data-gathering. At that point Charlie was looking animated and pleased. On the other hand, Charlene was withdrawing further and further into the woodwork. And then Charlie said, "Perhaps we should also talk a bit about what might happen if we have kids. We haven't made any specific decision about that, but that might be in the picture." As I nodded in wholehearted agreement, Charlene, who had been holding onto a little paperweight (the kind you can shake to see the snow fall) as if it were a crystal ball, shouted "No!" and flung the paperweight at her husband's chair. The paperweight ricocheted off the chair arm and careened to the floor. I looked down in alarm. My paperweight was safe. But Charlie had a broken pinky!

For me it was like the old raucous days of divorce mediation. But for Charlene it was very therapeutic. She started to cry and in utter despondency told us that she hated everything about the new house. She hated the thought of having to move to the suburbs, to take care of the house, to commute, to leave her friends, to leave the late-night dinners that the two of them shared after long office hours in the city. She hated the trees. Worst of all she hated the neighbors, and without much provocation would gladly shoot their dog. As she gained speed and momentum, I thought Charlie was going to fall into a dead faint. Needless to say, our conversation ended with our setting up an appointment to set goals, priorities, and procedures for financial decisions.

The most frequent money fights, and those luckily most easy to solve, are those involving Conflicting Priorities. There was really nothing wrong with the relationship between Charlie and Charlene except that they didn't agree with each other. First of all,

Charlene wanted a vacation, a stock and bond portfolio, and no residential realty. To her, home ownership was as good as death. She had no intention in her fast-paced advertising life to be stuck in the suburbs. Charlie was still holding on to the thought of a wife and kiddies and a white picket fence, even though in a million years he would never have been happy leading such a life. He wanted to rub his banisters and ring his doorbell. They also had a prenatal Kids vs. Us Syndrome. She didn't even want to be bothered with the thought; he was already planning for their college education.

In their own interesting way, they were both what I call Sunshine Kids. Neither of them was particularly financially oriented. She was creative and he was scientific. In many ways they didn't care about money as long as they had it. They painted with a broad brush, often overpaying just for convenience or time saved. Neither of them was a penny-pincher, and both of them were more than fair. And they both liked luxury and would gladly have given up the necessities for it.

In their general temperament and in their moods they were similar, yet on certain major goals they disagreed. I wanted to forestall long years of discomfort in a new home and unspoken resentment because of the move. However, they had signed the contract, and they both felt committed to the deal.

As a practical matter there were lots of things I could do for Charlie and Charlene. Many things can be done with a real estate contract. It can be flipped (sold to someone else), it can be closed and immediately placed on the market, and in extreme cases a minor penalty can be negotiated and the contract voided. If they wanted out, they could get out. But even so they must work on their priorities. They were perfect candidates for boardroom-instead-of-bedroom discussions of money. It was pointed out that residential real estate was a good idea for the couple. Their expensive monthly apartment wasn't doing much for their budget. Nevertheless, the $262,000 would not buy them a place that they would be happy with in Manhattan. They eventually found and purchased 5,000 square feet in another borough of New York (overlooking the water) in a community that is undergoing gentrification. Their place is gorgeous and certainly not suburban. Their priorities may change again, but if so they have a mechanism for admitting it and dealing with it. We also had them fund a wealth-building account, where they pay themselves first every single month after they fund their employee contribution plan. They'll be fine.

DASHED EXPECTATIONS

The problem of Dashed Expectations can be the cruelest of all. Many couples came together based on a certain set of expectations that never materialized. The woman may be disappointed because the husband did not meet her expectations of becoming a doctor (a prince). The man may be disappointed because he did not think he was marrying such a demanding woman, and yet that's just the way she turned out.

Sometimes it is not the couple themselves but the economy that has created the disappointment. This happens in the Inflation Babies Syndrome, where people have lost their sense of prosperity. Sometimes a third party has disappointed the couple, such as when an inheritance fails to come through (the Duke of Windsor Syndrome). Similarly, the wife often leaves the work force and relinquishes her career because of childbearing; the surprised husband may be disappointed, and thus they fight.

Expectations may be dashed when a couple compares themselves to seemingly more prosperous friends and family members, or media images that set up an extravagant, usually impossible lifestyle image. The new, higher living standards of the "Yuppies" (Young Urban Professionals) and "Tinks" (Two Incomes, No Kids)—the media darlings of the late 1980s—can make anyone feel like a failure if they harbor the least tendency toward self-doubt or insecurity. It's easy to feel that you're the only one who has not "arrived" in a culture that is so noisy about its money achievements. To understand how all the media glitz can make us feel about money and ourselves, let's take a look at one modern couple who began to think they were "downwardly mobile."

The POSSLQ (Persons of the Opposite Sex Sharing Living Quarters)

Rosalie and Jerry are unique clients for me. They are not married, and as far as I know they don't intend to be. Yet they have been living together for six years and are interdependent economically. They do their budgeting together and buy their luxuries together, and have both their names on their lease. Rosalie is thirty-seven years old and has been married before. She has one eight-year-old daughter who lives with her and Jerry; Jerry feels like a father to the child, having moved in with them when the little girl was two. Jerry has never been married, and he's about to turn forty.

They are looking for a house in the country that they could buy together, since they don't think they can afford a suburban home. Their fights take place all the time, they tell me. Nothing special precipitates them, but they are not getting anything done with respect to their financial planning.

Rosalie has been working for three years as a therapist, building a private practice. She also receives money from her former husband, Harry, for child support. She's entitled to accept spousal support under her agreement, but he never pays and she has never taken him to court. Jerry is the president of his own business. He manufactures power tools and has twenty employees. He's doing well but never feels secure and is always amazed at how much his overhead is escalating. He is beginning to feel that his fortunes are diminishing rather than growing.

Neither Rosalie nor Jerry came from a family with money. In fact, Jerry's father worked in a grocery store all his life, never owning it. Rosalie's father was a school janitor and a civil servant. Neither of their mothers worked. In both cases there were three children in the family.

Rosalie and Jerry can't believe that they are not doing as well as their parents did. They have found that while both their parents were able to afford fairly substantial homes in new neighborhoods when Rosalie and Jerry were children, neither of them can afford the kind of home they would like now. They are both college educated, and yet they don't seem to have that same feeling of prosperity as their parents.

Rosalie has been disappointed for some time over her first marriage, and Jerry has been disappointed over the fact that his business is not the million-dollar proposition that he expected it to be by the time he was forty years old.

All these Dashed Expectations result in intermittent, sometimes bitter, fighting over money. Rosalie has just started to work and has $35,000 in separate assets, which she got as part of her marital settlement. She also has a painting acquired during her marriage that is worth $15,000. She's making $25,000 in net fees from her clients and receives on a more or less steady basis 100 tax-free dollars a week for child support from Harry. He's also obligated to pay for her child's education and has a fund set aside for that. Jerry doesn't know what he earns. He knows that his business grosses $550,000 a year. But he has twenty employees whose salaries average $18,000 a year, he has ever-increasing rent on manufacturing space, he has everything from stationery and paper clips to telephone bills that have to be paid. Meanwhile, he's fallen into the habit of paying his personal bills, car expenses, and credit cards from the company's checkbook. His weekly cash draw is $300, all of which he seems to spend on eating out.

He has a Keogh plan to which he has contributed $15,000 a year since 1978. He also has $45,000 in bonds that he inherited from his mother.

I refused to help this couple until they made it absolutely clear whether they wanted separate or joint financial planning. I did not see them again for three months. They returned absolutely sure that they wanted joint planning. I then sent them back to keep a fight-pattern diary. The excerpts revealed that their fights took place two or three times a week (much more frequently than they suspected), and almost all were money oriented. All their fights were in their home; nearly all of them were in front of Rosalie's daughter. Because of this, they were guarded about what they said to each other.

The fights consisted mostly of cutting remarks from Rosalie about Jerry's inability to run his business and biting retorts from Jerry about Rosalie's pursuit of private clients and reluctance to accept a steady job with longer hours. They had both joint and separate checking accounts. They paid their bills haphazardly, often incurring late charges. Rosalie was resentful because Jerry had a secretary and yet never asked her to do any of their personal work. Jerry was resentful because he worked a much longer day than Rosalie and felt that she had more time to handle money matters.

It turned out after some discussion that the couple were just plain disappointed over how things had worked out. They had a sense of equality, they communicated quite well with regard to money, and their priorities were the same. They wanted to make more money and to have more financial freedom. But they were depressed. While they trusted each other and planned for fair dealing, and while they both had control over separate accounts, one from her former husband and the other from his mother, they sorely lacked a feeling of prosperity.

The couple got through the mechanics of the financial planning process very well. They committed themselves to the project of filing and preparing their net worth statements, cash flow calendars, and credit reports. The problem came when it was time to make money through investment decisions. Nothing appealed to them, because nothing would make them rich overnight. Nothing would make up to them for the fact that they had lived through an inflationary time and that they were not going to have the easy upward mobility that they expected by virtue of their college educations.

Once or twice Jerry almost invested his whole $45,000 in a speculative stock to see if he could really make it. Eventually, they implemented a small but well-balanced portfolio of mutual funds and a solid long-term retirement plan. I believe that had they had some couples counseling regarding their vast disappointments, they would have eventually embraced that program and gotten on their way despite their disappointments.

But after much analysis of their diaries and some solid thinking about their financial situation, the couple had a much better idea. Rosalie became involved in Jerry's business. In fact, she took the place of two employees, automatically increasing their income by $15,000 ($40,000 for the two employees minus her $25,000). She approached his business with an enthusiasm that he had long ago lost. But it was catching. Basically, she used her skills as a psychologist in office management. She also dealt differently with suppliers, and very differently with the books and records of the corporation. Within one year, business improved by 20 percent.

The couple accomplished what they wanted. They *found* a way to make more money. Because of this, within eighteen months they decided to take a slightly different approach to their financial plan than what I had originally suggested. It permitted them to buy the country house they were thinking of in the first place. An entirely new perspective was what this couple needed to stop fighting over money and make some.

FAILURE TO COMMUNICATE

Perhaps the most difficult problems for couples to deal with are those that involve a Failure to Communicate. For one reason or another these couples just cannot talk about money. She may act as the Poor Little Lamb and be so totally imbued with the belief that her femininity is coupled with an inability to understand money matters that she simply can't change. Often for women the *refusal* to handle money is a matter of pride and self-worth. "I'm loved, therefore I need not earn. Someone else takes care of me." Usually, however, it's expressed as a giggly admission of ignorance.

Sometimes one or the other partner just will not divulge important financial information. They will play the Rumpelstiltskin game. This is clearly the most serious syndrome, because it shows a lack of trust. Sometimes one uses the I've Got a Secret game because of a particular guilty secret, such as a gambling debt that has not been disclosed. This becomes easier to deal with as better communication and trust build. An insurmountable problem is faced when secretiveness hides adulterous conduct.

Indeed, while fault is not necessary to obtain a divorce in most states, adulterous conduct often becomes part of a money issue. Check stubs, credit cards, spending habits in general often reveal a clandestine relationship. In one of my divorce cases, extraordinary bills for breakfasts in hotels betrayed that the guilty husband was ordering for two. Hiding assets for this purpose will never be helped by financial planning, because the problem goes far deeper than money tension.

Another aspect that obscures communication is the plain fact that money fights can be a sexual stimulant. Ever since Adam and Eve, the best part of a good fight has been making up. If fighting is a stimulant to sex, why not fight about money? It's as good a topic as any other.

But at times the couple is *unaware* that their money fights are only the prelude to healthy sex, and starts to take them seriously. For now it is instructive to take your own survey and compare it with the results from your diary.

Silent Survey #10

Are the following statements true or false for you:

I fight more about money when I feel sexually satisfied than when I feel deprived.
Our fights over money are generally loud and violent but end in making up passionately.
Our money fights are often provoked when one of us wishes to *avoid* sex by creating animosity.

Money fights can be a way to stop sex or a way of initiating sex. When money problems result in an uproar, no one feels like having sex! It becomes a good excuse. Readers who can honestly identify their money fights as a substitute for voicing their sexual differences are already making progress. Often fighting about money feels safer than fighting about sex. Fortunately it's not necessary to resolve sex problems in order to stop fighting about money and make some.

The Doctor's Wife

At first glance, Julia seems to be the kind of woman many women envy, even if only secretly. She is attractive, her makeup is just right, her hair is glossy, and her diamond ring could light up a movie theater. Yet, a more unhappy woman I have never met. She came into my office alone for her first financial planning consultation. She brought with her a shopping bag full of papers and two handwritten looseleaf pages with a list of the family's assets and liabilities, and they were substantial.

Her husband Eric was a doctor on staff at a large urban hospital. He earned $120,000 per year plus a percentage of his private practice, some of which he paid back to the hospital in return for their absorption of his overhead expenses. All in all, from this and some insurance work he did, he had earned $225,000 a year for the past three years. Although he had earned considerably less before that, he hadn't earned under $100,000 for at least six years. They had two homes, a cooperative apartment in Manhattan, and an attractive country house in Connecticut. They also had a vacation condominium in Cancun, Mexico. A pension had been set up through the hospital for Eric, and he had encouraged Julia to keep her own bank account autonomously. Every once in a while he gave her a check for $25,000, and she had accumulated $150,000 over the years. All her money was in certificates of deposit that matured in anywhere from six months to three years. Julia had been putting documents together for two months in preparation for her meeting with me. In doing so, she learned that her husband had created a Clifford Trust for their two children that he had funded with $40,000 for each of them in 1976 (a year that she considered to be a particularly bad one financially for the two of them). He had never made any further contributions to the trust, as far as she knew. It also seemed that he had no will.

However, Eric did have an insurance policy of $300,000 (which Julia thought was very low). Julia had one on her life of $200,000. The couple had both joint and separate checking accounts. The joint accounts were funded by Eric every month or so when he put a substantial check into the bank. Julia had at least fifteen different credit cards, which she used at her discretion. There were four tax shelters that Eric had bought and that neither of them understood at all. It seemed, however, that Eric still owed $400,000 over a ten-year period to pay for these shelters. Otherwise, they had $75,000 in assorted stocks and bonds and another $60,000 in mutual funds. All these were held in an account in Eric's name.

Eric also kept a vault. Julia speculated that it must contain $200,000 in either cash, bearer bonds, or gold coins. This made her uneasy and angry at him for his secrecy. Julia worked one day a week for a decorator. She said it broke up her week. She had been, because of her decorating sources, able to amass a fairly nice collection of antiques and minor works of art.

When she came in to me to discuss money matters, Julia was considering a divorce. She wanted to protect herself in the event that she and Eric separated. She wanted to be sure that everything was in her name and that she would not be responsible for any of his tax manipulations, none of which she understood. On one hand, she told me that she knew nothing about the family finances, that she had "grabbed" every piece of paper she could find so that I could look through the so-called file and unravel sixteen years of material. On the other hand she seemed to have an iron-clad grasp of what every piece of furniture, the houses, and even her husband's pension plan was worth. She also informed me that no steps had been taken by either party toward a divorce. She just wanted to prepare herself for it. At the same time, she wanted to make good financial decisions that would benefit the couple in case they decided to stay married. She told me that Eric knew she had come and had refused to come with her, but had agreed at least verbally to go along with any transfer of assets to her name alone or joint names that I would recommend. Apparently she had threatened to leave him immediately if he didn't agree to this.

When I inquired as to the difficulty in the relationship, Julia told me that they were both having a midlife crisis. She gave me a long list of what seemed like rather minor offenses—no adultery, no abandonments, no cruelties (at least to the ear of a trained attorney)—over which she was very angry with Eric. The list did include such things as his being too wrapped up in his work, not taking any responsibility for the welfare of the children, not paying attention to money matters, and in general not treating her as an equal. I saw her many times after that, and I warmed to her as I got to know her better. Eventually, she confided that her sex life was unsatisfactory.

As a financial planner, I took a unique approach with Julia. I did prepare an organized net worth statement and liability statement for her. I advised her on the laws of inheritance, and referred her to an attorney who could advise her with respect to what her rights might be if there was a separation or divorce. Although my background is in that area, I didn't think it was appropriate to treat the matter as a divorce consultation; I felt it would interfere with my financial planning advice.

I also warned her that she could not walk a tightrope. Some decisions are best for the team money makers and some are best for her as an individual. For example, if I were to treat her $150,000 as a separate sum of money, I might wish to invest it for tax-free income. On the other hand, as a couple, the last thing they needed was income. Except for their real estate, most of which was residential, they had few growth-oriented investments. For a couple, the best investment would have been in conservative growth vehicles rather than certificates of deposit.

Over the next three months we constantly felt the tug-of-war between her emotional desires and her financial needs. Depending on whether the relationship was going well or poorly, she would come with a different demand. For example, during the three-month period, Eric gave her one of his $25,000 "contributions." She called me in a panic. Should she take it as usual, and if she did would she be acting as though she were accepting $25,000 every six months for support? She wondered if this was a trick.

During my consultations with her I never saw Eric. However, his presence was always felt. Occasionally I needed financial information, particularly about pensions or hospital staff benefits, that Julia did not have. I always felt free to call Eric's office, and the information was always duly sent me. I told him that financial plans are usually made in consultation with both parties, but under the circumstances I was drawing up the plan for the two of them. I explained that I understood they were having marital difficulties and that some of my advice would deal with division of assets in case there was a separation. I received a tidy typewritten letter from Eric telling me that he understood the matter completely and that not only could I go on with my work, but he would be happy to pay my bill. Never during the time that I worked with Julia did Eric ever call the office, make any inquiries, or attempt to speak with me directly.

Because of this lack of communication, it took me a little while to figure out what was wrong with the financial affairs of this relatively wealthy couple. And then it hit me: *they did not communicate.* Because they always had substantial funds, and because both of them considered the medical profession a financial end in itself, the couple had believed there was no need to discuss money. After all, Julia could have whatever she wanted, and her husband could handle the not inconsiderable remainder. Of course, there were hints of other syndromes—a touch of the Lolita Syndrome, for instance. However, Julia was not a whiner, nor did she particularly overspend. She certainly never put her husband in a position of having to work harder because of her spending. Nor was he a beast of burden. He managed his medical career very well and enjoyed the good life (golf, a nice car, a good country club) as much as his wife did. Any time there's a difference in earnings and the husband is the major earner, one can usually spot some of the Breadwinner Syndrome or Doll's House Syndrome with the husband handling the lion's share of the money. But there was no feeling of Inequality. Despite the fact that the marriage was on the rocks, there seemed to be a great deal of mutual respect in this relationship. Neither of them had Dashed Expectations. On the contrary, their expectations had largely been fulfilled. Nor did their priorities differ. They both wanted everything, and as a team they had the means for it. In fact, it was only because Julia was in danger of not receiving everything due her in the event of a bitter divorce that she wanted to do financial planning in the first place.

The problem was indeed with communication. The couple displayed a touch of many of the syndromes under this base problem. Despite Eric's willingness to provide information, there was always the feeling that something had been hidden. Perhaps it was just the money in the vault, and perhaps Julia was wrong about the amount. But it was never wholly disclosed to our office. Further, a look at some past tax returns showed losses from several enterprises of which Julia was unaware, as well as reported foreign income that surprised Julia even further.

On the other hand, Julia's passive aggression regarding her ability to handle money made it almost impossible for Eric to communicate with her. In fact, in working with her I could see the trouble Eric may have had trying to include her in his financial planning. She would alternately bemoan her inability to understand money matters, her math phobia, her boredom with the topic (what a Poor Little Lamb). On the other hand, she would demand exact calculations, often to the penny, of anything that her husband had. She was very frustrated by the fact that the values of stocks, bonds, and shares in mutual funds fluctuate, and that a financial statement might be slightly outdated by the time it was received. Julia wanted to know about money, but she secretly resented having to put in any effort. It made it difficult to communicate with her.

But despite anything one could say about Julia, Eric's transgressions were far worse. He seemed to have the attitude that he was in so much control that he could let Julia do any type of dance she wished with regard to money. If it turned out to be what he expected, he would go along with it. If it didn't, he would simply stonewall and do nothing. Unquestionably this went on throughout the marriage. On the surface he was open and gave her information when asked. But, in fact, his secretary probably knew more about his finances than his wife. He kept his own counsel, and at times I even suspected he had an accountant other than the one that Julia knew as the family accountant.

Eventually, the matter became one for the divorce court and not for the financial planner. Attitudes of trust, fair dealing, autonomy, and even prosperity had become deeply distorted. Julia certainly didn't trust Eric to tell the truth, and Eric certainly wasn't telling everything. Even Julia's autonomy, measured by a hefty $150,000 bank account, felt to Julia like a "payoff" from Eric to keep her nose out of his business. While the couple never seriously worried about money for survival, they had lost the feeling of prosperity that they needed to keep them striving together.

How much happier I would have been if I could have done some financial planning for Julia and Eric as an intact, upper-income couple. Indulge me while I give you a quick analysis of what might have been had I worked on the case, based on my work with a similarly situated couple who had a good marriage.

First, I would have talked with them about serious short-term and long-term goal planning. This couple had enough money not to do penny-point budgeting or worry much about their liabilities. In fact, they had too little debt service. I probably would have had them refinance their homes, getting a lower rate of interest and freeing up a great deal of equity. That money in turn would have been invested in income-producing real estate that would have paid off the loan and appreciated in value at the same

Financial Planning Steps	Most Damaging Base Problem	Formula for Success
Record keeping	Conflicting Priorities Failure to Communicate	Systemized boardroom record keeping
Setting goals	Failure to Communicate Dashed Expectations	Setting goals separately and resolving conflicts
Determining cash flow	Inequality Failure to Communicate	Using a cash flow calendar to reveal cash flow information
Budgeting	Failure to Communicate Dashed Expectations	Preparing a pay-yourself-first budget with immediate gratification
Making investment decisions	Failure to Communicate Conflicting Priorities Inequality	Precision calculation of future results
Calculating net worth	Dashed Expectations Failure to Communicate	Graded net worth targeted to eliminate useless assets
Improving credit and controlling debts	Inequality Failure to Communicate	Discussing a uniform philosophy and setting up good record keeping
Risk Management (Insurance)	Conflicting Priorities	Calculating minimum needs and finding least expensive alternatives
Housing	Failure to Communicate Conflicting Priorities	Learning how to make your most long term investment—a precedence
Tax Planning	Conflicting Priorities Failure to Communicate	Contracting out for best data

time. While such real estate is difficult to find (how do you make armadillo soup? It's easy, but first you have to find an armadillo), if you devote enough time to it, it can be found. This would have started Eric on the road to an independent income separate from his medical practice.

If either of them had any particular hopes and dreams (traveling around the world, retiring early, you name it), we could have worked on that and built it into their financial picture. In other words, they would have taken a step beyond the country club and into the fulfillment of some really spectacular goals. Furthermore, they could have worked on autonomy together, within their working relationship. Very possibly Eric needed to withhold some of the details, and as long as Julia felt protected with substantial joint and separate assets, the relationship might have worked. But communication was insufficient. Better tax planning was also a key to less anxiety on Eric's part. I had seen him make at least three mistakes in his tax dealings, first with some shoddy tax shelters, and again with excess payment on foreign income. What he needed was sophisticated, accurate, and legitimate planning. He had an unspoken desire that I could never cure to be shrewd rather than right when it came to money planning, particularly since he was unwilling even to participate in the process.

There is a definite relationship between the syndrome types and the standard techniques for money management that can be used to alleviate them. Take a look at the chart on the opposite page to see how they are connected.

We will be talking more about the specific money management techniques that can remedy many of these base problems in the last chapter of this book. These techniques are very easy to understand and use, but at times can result in such a change in the relationship and how a couple interacts that some tension may be inevitable at first. Therefore, some tips on conflict resolution may be needed before you attempt to apply them.

III
MAKING PEACE

6

Conflict Resolution

I F making money was purely unemotional, simply learning money management techniques would be sufficient
to achieve success. But most financial decisions are made in an
atmosphere of personal as well as economic insecurity, and so
conflict-resolution techniques play an almost equally important role.

This is not a therapy manual; the goal of this book is not (and
could never be) to solve all the underlying problems in a relationship, but rather for the couple who reads it to stop fighting about
money and make some. Without the money-fight mechanism as a
means of expression, their troubles will find other outlets, pref-
erably more constructive ones. But if these other outlets become
destructive or troublesome enough, the couple may need to seek
professional counseling.

I've done my best to make this chapter appropriate for use by
couples rather than by labor unions, corporations, and business

partnerships, from which conflict-resolution techniques are derived. Through years of negotiating on behalf of business clients and businesses, I have gained one important insight that is even more significant in the area of couples conflict resolution: No matter how complex the fight and no matter what the outcome, it is possible for the parties to continue to meet and work together. I have rarely seen a dispute, no matter how major and no matter how emotionally draining, result in a permanent split. This does not mean that labor unions don't strike, that businesses don't compete, and that partnerships don't dissolve. But by and large, even with intense conflict these entities live to fight another day.

I am also amazed and sometimes amused at the ongoing relationship that these worthy opponents have with each other. For example, the attorneys for labor are frequently friendly with the attorneys for management outside of business. Yet they do not give in to the other's demands out of friendship when they act as advocates. How is this possible? It is possible because they act in a manner that may be psychologically artificial, but that works when it comes to conflict resolution.

WEARING TWO HATS

This is the first conflict-resolution attitude for a couple to adopt. You may be angry, you may be sexually frustrated that day, the kids may have gotten on your nerves, but when you're dealing with money you must wear a different hat. My great friend and colleague from chapter 1 (the one who hadn't had a money fight for thirty-eight years) was talking to me one day about how hard it was to be a wife, mother, and career person. She told me of a friend who literally wore a hat when she wanted to be left alone. She informed her maid, her kids, her husband, and her mother, "Don't bother me when I'm wearing this hat. It means I need to be alone." As eccentric as that may seem, it's not a bad idea. Anything you do that helps you act as business people rather than as a feuding couple will help. This is the whole concept of the boardroom atmosphere.

As the boardroom is adopted by a couple as their *sole* financial planning environment, they develop a "boardroom response." If you've ever walked into a special place of quiet (a church, a massage room, a barber shop, a library), you may have felt a quieting response. This was a place where you felt safe and happy. This happens with the boardroom, too, except that the feeling is one of businesslike productivity. Many couples literally leave their conflicts outside the door of the boardroom and begin to work in tandem, even if it has to be done in an artificial manner. Once they enter that room at the appointed time, they speak only about money matters, not about anything else. This allows them to turn immediately to their boardroom agenda and get to work.

LISTENING

Listening is the most significant method of conflict resolution you can ever learn. It's also the toughest. Because we have so much to say, and so much to argue about, we tend to talk. Talk is cheap, and can keep us poor. A premium should be placed on the art of listening. I hear that many corporations even teach their executives how to listen.

Take turns listening. If one partner has something to say, the other must quietly sit back and pay attention. If you're so agitated that you can't listen, force yourself to write down what's being said as the other speaks. Pretend you are going to be quizzed on comprehension when the other party is finished. Then think over their words in your mind before you speak. When you do speak, do so only to ask your mate to refine what they meant or explain exactly what they had in mind in the event you don't understand one or two points. In very difficult conflict-resolution negotiations such as those between labor and management, there may even be a session where only one party makes a presentation. After that everybody goes home. That's all that's been accomplished.

One party got to say what they wanted without the other responding. In the next session the other party gets a chance to speak. You might even draw straws to decide who goes first.

After both partners have had a chance to express why they want a money matter to be approached in a certain way, they should then write down their reasons as succinctly as possible. They should also write down what they think the result of their decision will be.

Somewhere along the line, one of two things will happen. Either one party will agree with the other and change his or her mind, or neither will change their mind. In the latter case, the next technique must be employed.

COMPROMISE

If neither changes their mind, the next technique of choice is *compromise*. My five-year-old son calls it "making a deal." And that's exactly what it is. Within the context of a particular issue (whether to buy a new car, for example), a compromise must be approached. To do this, one must make a compromise proposal.

The proposal might, for example, suggest that a car should be bought, but that it should first be leased or rented for a short period to see whether it's really needed and how much it enhances the lifestyle of the couple.

Which one compromises first? If you can't agree, toss a coin. In business negotiation there is costly and time-consuming posturing over who makes the offer first. Forget it. Just get the show on the road.

All compromises should be couched in the context of the issue itself. If the couple is fighting over whether the husband should retire early, the compromise should deal with the issue of retirement. Only if no compromise can be made in the context of the issue itself should extraneous matters be brought in. A deal that compromises two completely separate points often feels unsatisfactory to both parties. The bigger these issues are—e.g., whether to retire or where to live—the more unhappy the compromise is and the less workable it will be when the parties leave the board-room.

Don't confuse compromise with "giving in." If you always feel you get the short end of the stick, examine yourself first. Feelings of dignity and self-respect come from within. They are not be-stowed by the other party. I have seen lawyers, particularly women and particularly young ones, leave a negotiation feeling defeated and outmaneuvered. I have seen brash macho young men leave a negotiation feeling like the cock of the roost. Yet objectively they may have done equally well, or the woman may have done better. If you feel you must be 100 percent victorious to have any power at all, you'll always feel defeated by any compromise. Oddly enough, people who feel least powerful often demand more and compromise less. When they make a deal they usually do not feel they have done so with dignity. Instead they feel they have "given in."

Of course, each teammate must treat the other spouse with dignity and expect the same for himself or herself. If one does give in, the other has no business saying, "I told you so." You are in this together. This is team money making. Remember that when business opponents compromise, they really do have different needs and different agendas. Usually, what's good for one is bad for the other, and they have made a true compromise. In team money making you both have the same goal: to enhance both parties' financial security.

Once you develop the technique, it becomes easier to compro-mise. As you practice the 10-Step Method, you will be dealing more and more from a position of knowledge regarding your money. It will become clearer to the two of you what's right and what's wrong for you. There will be fewer questions, less debate, and less divisiveness.

If no compromise can take place in the context of the issue under discussion, then you must engage in the third technique.

113

ALTERNATING VICTORIES

This is a fancy way of saying *taking turns*. For example, one of you may wish to take a $5,000 chance on a new stock, and the other may be too conservative. Since neither can tell the future, there is no *right* answer and the subject becomes a matter for conflict. When conflict is so clear-cut, the parties should take turns getting what they want. This is much easier for a couple than it is for businesses and unions, where issues are much more complicated. The advantage you have as a couple over any other negotiating group is that each of you works autonomously. This means that neither of you has a committee that you have to go back to for approval. There is less *politics* in couple compromise and conflict resolution than in any other type.

Taking turns gives a feeling of equality between the parties and equality of issues. If she gets a special coat this year, he should get a vacation next year. If they take a chance on the stock (his idea), she'll get the coat. As long as the budget can afford the item in the first place, it becomes a matter of taking turns as to which one gets what they wish. Such an exercise enhances feelings of fundamental fairness that are important in money making and attacks the inequality problem at its core. If you can't afford to take turns, try a closely related technique: meeting minimal goals.

MEETING MINIMAL GOALS

If the problems are in the realm of spending versus saving, luxuries versus necessities, or any of the other priority conflicts, this technique can work like a charm. Take the example of the Now vs. Later Syndrome. One of you wants immediate gratification, the other would like to save for the future.

By compromising on minimal security goals that must be taken care of, the couple can agree that the remainder of the fund will be used to "play with." Don wants to go on an expensive vacation. Barbara is angry and upset because in her view they never save. She sets a yearly goal of $3,000 in savings and insists that they fund their IRA and put the rest in a growing money-market account. Don, however, wants immediate gratification. Barbara agrees that as long as these minimal goals are met, the vacation money can be borrowed and the debt service made part of their fixed budget. He can get his special treat. As long as Don also feels that these minimal goals benefit him, he will probably go along with them. Each gets some of what they want.

If you have tried all these methods and still can't agree, you may simply not have enough information. This brings us to the next technique.

DATA GATHERING

Most people don't realize how ignorant they are about their money and how often they can't make decisions because of their ignorance. If they had the facts, they'd know the answer. If they knew the answer, they would see that there is only one correct answer for the two of them, and they wouldn't fight. Unfortunately, it's easier (and more interesting) to fight than it is to review a tax return. Nevertheless, data gathering is a significant and essential part of conflict resolution. A good executive—and that's what you are when you are managing your own money—has the facts.

Sometimes a dispute arises over who does the data gathering. This is particularly the case when Inequality is the problem between the couple. It is difficult to know which way the pendulum will swing; will the person with greater or lesser power be given the task? With some couples, the powerless one is given the dirty job of data gathering. In cases where lack of communication has been a problem, the more powerful partner may insist on doing the data gathering in an attempt to obscure or hide facts. If task allocation is your problem, review the task allocation section in Chapter 1.

If both parties simply refuse to do the job, the problem should be solved either by taking turns or by adopting another method of conflict resolution, one that I consider useful only as a last resort.

CONTRACTS

I'm far from committed to the use of written contracts between couples. Nevertheless, as a member of the advisory board of *New Marriage* magazine, I'm aware of the keen interest in antenuptial agreements and couples contracts.

As an attorney I have prepared these agreements when people have unequal wealth from a first marriage or an inheritance. Second-marriage premarital agreements aren't bad and can put everyone on notice of the intention of each with respect to their money. But beware of the chilling effect on personal relationships of iron-clad contracts. Still, with all the chill in the air over finances these days, and all the fears caused by alimony, galimony, and palimony, antenuptial agreements are having a heyday. Mind you, the word is *ante*, meaning coming before or prior to, not *anti*, meaning against or adverse to. These are agreements that couples have traditionally signed prior to a marriage in order to define the financial arrangements they will have throughout the years. But antenuptial agreements can be signed during the marriage as well.

A true antenuptial agreement is a contract signed by both parties and notarized. In most states it is acknowledged as if it were a deed. It need not be filed with the court. The contract relates exactly how the parties will hold property during the course of their marriage. It also frequently waives any rights of inheritance that a partner may have. To cap it off, there can be and frequently is a release of any spousal or marital share in the other's estate.

This means that when one spouse dies, the other doesn't inherit anything at all unless that spouse has been left money or some specific items in a will.

This supersedes the law in effect in almost every state that requires a person to leave some of his or her wealth to the surviving spouse, unless there has been a divorce or a formal separation. In some states the estate of a deceased person is even permitted to carry on a divorce proceeding that has been commenced in order to prevent the surviving spouse from inheriting. But if there has been no formal proceeding, a spouse is entitled to inherit no matter what the deceased wanted.

One useful role of the antenuptial agreement is to protect children of a first marriage in the event of a second marriage. Those of you who are newly divorced may or may not be heartened to know that you are eight times more likely to marry than someone who has never been married at all. People who have married once generally like the institution of marriage, even if they didn't like their cellmate. Because there are so many second marriages, many of them very successful, antenuptial agreements are being reconsidered and are certainly becoming more popular.

Second marriages, particularly later in life, often do not serve the purpose of making the couple an economic unit, striving together for a lifetime of financial upward mobility. Rather, both partners are usually settled into their financial lifestyles; they want to preserve what they have achieved and to protect their children. They are always afraid that the second marriage may not work out; if that happens, they don't want to add financial pain to the emotional pain.

The antenuptial agreement is ideal. It waives any rights that each spouse must under state law give to the other in their estate; yet it permits either spouse voluntarily to leave to the other as much as he or she wishes. If there is an ongoing business or other important income producer, the agreement can state who shall run the business or handle the investments and who shall receive the income or proceeds from it. The agreement can state that funds from a certain source belong to both parties equally or in different proportions. The parties can even agree on how they will spend certain sums throughout the course of the marriage.

Formal contracts are best left for important major issues that can be isolated. If a minor issue arises, a written agreement can cause problems. After all, there's no need to kill a flea with an elephant gun! Use the written boardroom bylaws instead. For example, if the dispute is over who is going to do data gathering, prepare the weekly boardroom agenda, or remember to fund the IRA, you are much better off writing down your "deal" informally if it needs to be written at all.

Nevertheless, you may find that even after years of being together you would be best off with a formal contract between you. This is particularly true if one of you would like to maintain some autonomy and you find that this has become the fundamental problem. If you are not "allowed" to have money that you handle yourself, if you must combine everything, an agreement can work. If one member of the couple has exceeded the other in earnings, creating Dashed Expectations, there can be serious danger of splitting up. Sometimes this resentment can be alleviated by a written agreement stating that the higher earner is autonomous with respect to his or her earnings from a separate job or business. Feelings of trust and fair dealing must be preserved, and the agreement must be workable and not strained. Frequently these feelings go out the window as soon as negotiation begins. Nevertheless, if you have come to the conclusion that a written agreement is what you want, there is one cardinal rule to follow.

Deal only with specific issues. If the issue is vague it ends up being nothing more than an umbrella under which you have to decide every issue in your finances before you even get started making money.

If you have reached the stage of making contracts, you may need mediation rather than conflict resolution. If so, you should consider the final procedure of calling in a third party.

THIRD-PARTY INTERVENTION

Trade associations, businesses, partnerships, and labor/ management often call in a mediator or arbitrator to help them solve a particularly thorny problem. You may have to also. When used too often, this technique becomes expensive and interferes with the 10-Step Method, which requires you to work as a team on a regular basis. Nevertheless, as long as you don't confuse the kind of third-party help I am suggesting with couples therapy, you'll still be able to stay on the right track. Couples therapy is an ongoing process. The procedure is very important. Feeling better and alleviating strain is one of its goals. The pace of couples therapy can be long and drawn out and still be successful. This is not true of money making and financial planning. Financial planning and money making must have immediate results. Things have to get done quickly. Economics does not wait for you to work out your libidinal frustration or the bad relationship you had with your mother. If you can't pay your bills, you've got to do something fast. If labor/management had first to iron out a hundred years' worth of political differences before they could make an agreement, the whole country would be on strike.

The type of third-party intervention I'm suggesting is *issue specific*. When you have boiled down your problems to their specifics, gathered all the information you need, listened to both sides, tried to compromise, tried to make a deal on separate issues, and tried to make a contract, and all these steps have failed, you have come to what I call a *true impasse on a specific issue*. In that case, call in a third party.

If you don't want to make an expensive proposition out of this, call on a friend or relative. If you think you need more objective professional help, go to a fee-paid financial planner and specifically state the issue and the disagreement. You will get a highly objective insight. If there's a substantial amount of money involved, you might want to hand over the problem to a money manager who will charge you based on a percentage of the money that he or she is handling for you. If the problem is one of management rather than investment (such as budgeting or cash flow), then you want a financial planner to prepare a report that can help you with the problem. If the issue is fairness (both of you feel the other is being unfair), your accountant, investment attorney, or even relative will do.

At this stage, let me introduce you to a special method of impasse mediation that can work very well when couples use a third party.

Sydelle and Harold have a tough problem. Sydelle has been counting on inheriting a great deal of money from her father. Harold didn't marry her for her money, but the eventual inheritance was always a fact of life for them. They dealt with their finances accordingly. They spent too much and didn't expect to have to rely on their own finances entirely. Things went quite well. In fact, her father gave them money for a down payment on a home and substantial Christmas gifts each year, which they used for vacations and occasionally for the children's tuition. Sydelle never worked. Harold started his own business.

Had they not expected her inheritance, he would have worked for a corporation with a much more secure job. Instead, he had the opportunity to follow his dream. Surprisingly, when Sydelle's father died, he left her the sum she expected, but as trust income only. There was no lump sum forthcoming at the time of his death. This dashed the expectations that the couple had of expanding Harold's business. Harold insisted that Sydelle demand the trustee (her uncle) release principal from the trust. If he refused, Harold wanted Sydelle to co-sign a substantial business loan. The more he insisted on these demands, the more she tightened her control over the trust income that was sent to her quarterly. Their fights have been increasing for over a year now.

What was once a happy family has been radically changed by Dashed Expectations regarding inheritance. In fact, Harold is on very shaky terms with Sydelle's siblings and with her family as a whole. Harold is strained by having to fend for his family by himself. Most people will not feel sympathetic to this problem, and will assert that Harold's "free ride" is simply over. But for the couple, a difficult burden was placed on the marriage.

The couple have tried to work together and have made compromises on all issues except invasion of principal. Harold believes that Sydelle has no faith in his business ability. She believes that her father, now dead, has been protecting her from her husband all along. Things are getting rough.

Impasse mediation could work for them. A third party would be chosen, and each spouse would bring in a *proposal*. The impasse mediator would have the absolute right to choose one or the other proposal. There would be no compromise, nor would the impasse mediator make any suggestions. He or she would listen to all the facts, ask questions, and then choose from what he or she considered to be the fairer of the two proposals and the better of the two for the family as a whole. Accordingly, each side is forced to create a proposal couched in terms of fairness for both. How much could each really give up and still live with the situation? If Sydelle concludes that her only proposal is not to invade, she runs the risk that a compromise proposal by the husband will seem fairer to the mediator and will be accepted. Harold is in the same spot.

For very minor issues, couples may wish to do this without a third party. Each can write down their fairest compromise. Pick the solution from a hat and stick to it. This is a good exercise in fair dealing.

The following is a list of the conflict-resolution techniques and the base problems most helped by their proper use.

Compromise Device	*Problem Most Helped*
Listening	Inequality
Compromising with dignity	Conflicting priorities, Inequality
Alternating victories	Conflicting priorities, Inequality

Compromise Device	*Problem Most Helped*
Meeting minimum goals	Conflicting priorities, Dashed Expectations
Data gathering	Inequality, Failure to Communicate
Contracts	Inequality, Failure to Communicate, Conflicting Priorities
Third parties	All conflicts when absolutely necessary

The tools for success in team money making involve interactive worksheets, data-gathering questionnaires, and decision making that requires direct participation from you and your mate. Even if one team member is willing to assume the obligation of preparing the material, the other must still cooperate in sharing information and in making final decisions.

To further permit the *organized* use of those tools I have combined them in a 10-step process, each step building on the one before. These steps to complete financial control truly help you make money instead of war. The 10-Step Method is not therapy, although it is therapeutic. It is actually a form of behavior modification.

While changes in behavior alone are not enough to heal the problem underlying the fight pattern, they are often enough to help make money. This positive step—whether it culminates in paying a debt, saving for retirement, or taking a vacation—lessens monetary stress and permits the *true* cause of the fighting to be explored in more traditional therapeutic settings.

7

The 10-Step Method for Successful Team Money Making

Y OU are about to begin the 10-Step Method. If you have followed the instructions in chapter 1, you have already gathered most of the data you'll need, or at least know where to find it. You have set your boardroom location and set a time and place for your first meeting. If you are working alone, you'll probably be doing so up until the point that investment decisions actually have to be made and possibly even after. If you are working in concert, Step 1, Record Keeping, will be your first experience in joint money management. Don't skip steps, and don't cheat. If the process takes you longer than expected, so be it. On the other hand, if you feel absolutely hopeless about getting through one of the steps (Record Keeping is usually the worst), don't feel guilty about it. Cut through the tedium and get to the point as fast as you can.

Remember, the 10-Step Method is simple, sometimes deceptively so. It's hard to believe that just gathering data and making decisions can change your life. Take the leap of faith, it works! Once again, here are the 10 steps:

STEP 1: Record Keeping
STEP 2: Goal Setting
STEP 3: Determining Cash Flow
STEP 4: Budgeting
STEP 5: Calculating Net Worth
STEP 6: Investment Planning
STEP 7: Handling Credit
STEP 8: Insurance
STEP 9: Housing
STEP 10: Tax Planning

As you read through this list, focus on the areas in which you are most interested. Identify those steps you expect will be most troubling to you. You can pace each step differently, and work together on some, separately on others. But before you go any further, do the following brief exercise.

FINANCIAL WARMUP

This little questionnaire will give you a good laugh at yourself and may provide some motivation to practice the 10-Step Method. Answer quickly, write down the first answer that comes to your mind ("I don't know" is the most common one). Do not look up the answers until you have completed the test. When you do look up the answers, write down how long it took to gather the information. Are your books and records in disarray? Do you have the name or number of the proper professionals to call? If you are so out of control that you can't look up the answers quickly, don't. Just continue through the 10-Step Method—you will know the answers by the end of it.

Quick—Write Down:
- The name and address of your lawyer.
- Your yearly fuel bill—if no fuel bill use electric, telephone, etc.
- Your legal next of kin.
- How much interest is charged if you borrow against your insurance policy.
- The amount of monthly retirement income you'll have from your corporate or other pension plan if you retire at age sixty-five.
- The amount deducted from your paycheck for federal income tax (for the self-employed, the amount of your estimated income tax in the last quarter).
- The maturity date of bonds you hold; where it applies, the interest given by your bank or money market fund.
- The monthly cost of your checking account.
- The definition of a trust.
- The present price of gold.
- Your spouse's net income.
- The amount in taxes you paid last year.
- The going rate in your neighborhood for lawn mowing, dog walking, garbage removal.
- The amount you must set aside each year to send your kids to college.
- The dollar value of the sale of your most prized material possession.
- The rental value of your home.
- The difference between a mutual and a money market fund.
- The physical location of your last five years of income tax returns.
- The cost to make a directory-assisted phone call.
- Your income tax bracket.

How did you do? Don't be surprised if you know little about your present finances—few people do.

Think about, and if the atmosphere permits, talk about, your own financial histories. Take a verbal survey with your mate (the way you've been doing your Silent Surveys earlier in the book) by discussing the following questions and statements concerning your financial history:

My parents spoke often of money management.
My parents taught me to earn money, not to invest money.
My parents taught me to marry money, not to earn it.
My parents never taught me anything about money.
My parents were financially astute.
My parents were financially secretive.
When I was a kid I thought I was rich (poor).
I worked when I was a kid.
I first began to worry about money when I was (age).
The best thing I ever did with my money before I was twenty-one was:
The best thing I ever did with my money after I was twenty-one was:
My biggest financial failures have been because of action (inaction).

STEP 1: RECORD KEEPING

I have found the single greatest stumbling block to complete financial control to be organized record keeping. When your shopping bag breaks, you know you need a new filing system! Step 1 will help you (force you) to get organized. Record keeping consists of (1) organizing important papers; (2) reconciling statements; and (3) extrapolating significant financial data from those statements. Let's consider each of these.

Organizing Important Papers

Begin by locating important documents. Primary examples are:

- Birth certificate
- Life insurance policies
- Other insurance policies
- Stocks
- Bonds
- Notes or mortgages receivable
- Deeds
- Leases
- Will or other testamentary documents
- Wills of family members, if pertinent
- Trust instruments
- Pension, profit-sharing, and other retirement plans
- Cemetery deeds, real estate deeds, evidence of cooperative or condominium ownership
- Employment contracts
- Employee benefit plan statements
- Partnership agreements, shareholders' agreement
- Closely held corporation buy-sell agreements
- Divorce decrees and/or separation agreements
- Marriage contracts
- Marriage certificate

Keep these documents in one place in your home or a safe deposit box. If necessary leave them in a savings-bank vault, but this is not my favorite choice, because a court order is usually necessary to open a vault in the event of death.

Next, create a space in your boardroom for a filing system for papers you will be working with regularly. You are going to need enough room for your money market and brokerage statements, check stubs, tax returns, and more. Needless to say, make the filing process as entertaining as you can, because you are going to be working with these documents on a weekly basis. Colorful file folders, extension folders, and labels are indulgences worth the money if they appeal to you.

Remember that a personal filing system is absolutely necessary. I know you'd prefer to buy Japanese yen or waterfront property in Nova Scotia and thereby grow rich. But the truth is that rich people become that way by being organized about their money. You'll need a filing system to back up your business deductions, challenge an incorrect bank or brokerage statement, avoid tax filing extensions or learn when to apply for them, keep track of the yield and maturity dates of your investments, and even to keep track of how much you earn. You are welcome to devise your own system; I have found that the following nine categories of documents, each with their own file folder and many of them with subdivisions, work for most people:

1. Unpaid monthly bills where a late charge is incurred
2. Unpaid monthly bills where cancellation can occur if unpaid
3. Unpaid monthly bills where some other type of penalty is imposed
4. All other unpaid monthly bills
5. Paid bills not useful to document tax deductions (kept from one to three years depending on space and availability of canceled checks to prove payment
6. Paid bills useful to document tax deductions. Possible subdivisions:
   a. related to business expenses
   b. related to ownership of real property; co-op certificate
   c. related to medical expenses
   d. related to child care
   e. related to alimony/maintenance
   f. related to sales tax
   g. related to interest on loans
7. Income statements from outside sources: W2, 1099, K1
8. Monthly asset statements
   a. bank statements
   b. brokerage
   c. financial planner or money manager
   d. pension
   e. insurance

Plus an updated Estimate of Monthly Cash Flow (see page 140).

9. All completed income tax returns from forever (how many can you have—120?).

Once you have structured your files and set a place for them in your home, you must keep the filing up to date. It's a mechanical task that should be done weekly, or at least bimonthly. Successful couples don't fight over record-keeping task allocation, but they do gripe about it. If this is your problem, sit at the boardroom table and make a list of who is going to do what. Here's an example:

- He will have all the insurance policies gathered with a list of the death benefits, cash surrender value, loans against the policy, and rate of loans by (date).
- He will speak with his personnel officer and have the data on his pension by (date).
- He will balance the checkbook and do the net worth and liability tallying every other month, alternating with her.
- She will call all the brokers for their latest statement of assets by (date).
- She will search the drawers for the marriage certificate, latest will, and all the past tax returns she can find.

For those of you who find filing an insurmountable stumbling block, try to integrate it into your office work if either of you has a secretary able to take care of personal things. You may want to discuss equipment such as calculators or a personal home computer. If you really want to spend some money, bring your "shopping bag" to a financial planner, who on a fee-paid basis will organize your papers for you. She will give you a computerized list of your income assets and taxes and create a filing system for you, but at a price.

If the job seems hopeless, the best thing you can do is start from today. Instead of filing old papers and ending up with a time-consuming project, just get started! Prepare nine empty folders with the nine categories I have outlined. As statements come in, file them. You'll have a working filing system after the first thirty days. Make phone calls to get the following information immediately: your bank balances, brokerage balances, amount left on loans, and pension benefits. Just about everything else will come in to you on a statement of some type within the next thirty days. If you can gather up past tax returns and receipts for tax-deductible items, your filing system will be complete.

Reconciling Statements

Monthly reconciliations (even every two months is OK) of your bank statements, investment statements, and loan statements must be made. To reconcile your bank statements, arrange canceled checks in numerical order and list missing numbers to indicate checks that have not yet cleared. Cross off the checks you have before you on your statement and checkbook. Any transactions that have been made that do not appear on your bank statement must be tallied to arrive at your current balance. Don't forget to check late charges and interest credited to you on interest-paying accounts. Be sure your deposit slips reconcile with the bank's entries. (For a step-by-step method of mathematical calculation, see Stephanie Winston's book, *Getting Organized.*)

This is also the time to reconcile investment statements. A typical mutual fund statement will show you how many new shares you have acquired by reinvesting your dividends or interest. A typical consolidated statement will show you a variety of transactions that took place the month before. A typical stock statement will show you transfers, sales, and loan transactions. If you are hopelessly lost, you *must* meet with your banker or broker for an explanation.

Next, reconcile your loan statements. Be sure your loan, both principal and interest, has been reduced by the amounts paid. Note any change of interest due to variable interest rates. (See Step 7, Handling Credit, to understand these better.) Finally, on a monthly basis, pay your bills. Pay those bills that incur penalties and cancellations first. But even before that, pay yourself! (See the section on the Pay Yourself First Budget beginning on page 144 to understand the importance of this step.)

Unquestionably, this is a lot of work. But do it, even if you must do it all yourself. Sure, it means more work for you, but it may also mean more power.

As you create your filing and reconciliation system, you will begin to see why I maintain that the issue of inequality is alleviated greatly through record keeping. Knowledge is power, and the balance of power will be in the lap of the one who knows about the family finances. Keeping someone ignorant about their own money is a time-honored technique of keeping them powerless. Record keeping also has a salutary effect on communication problems. It's difficult to be secretive and refuse to talk about money when your data and filing system are so explicit.

Extrapolating Significant Financial Data

Filing papers and reconciling statements are only stages in the record-keeping process. Extrapolating from those files is another. Some documents contain secrets like your *net worth*, liability statement, budget, and insurance needs. All are so important that a separate step is devoted to each.

It is a good idea to update your net worth statement every three months and your liability statement yearly. Many people keep a running total of their tax deductions. This is fine for those who enjoy it and are organized; others may just keep their receipts and have their accountant do the rest. Remember, there is no glory in keeping your own records. There is only trouble in not having records at all, or not keeping them straight.

A Final Word About Record Keeping . . .

As a couple you may wish to keep records together or separately. As long as it doesn't cause problems in task allocation, you'll make the same amount of money no matter who does the tedious work. Act without rancor or accusation. Never leave record keeping undone out of spite. If it's his turn to keep the checkbook tallied and he was watching the football game instead, you won't make money by letting it go until it becomes an uncontrollable mess. Do it yourself and deal with task allocation at the next boardroom meeting.

Step 1: Record Keeping Task Synopsis

- Gather 20 significant documents.
- Buy file folders and labels.
- File unfiled papers or decide to start from today.
- Set monthly date for reconciliation of statements.
- Reconcile to the present or decide to start from today.
- Set monthly date to pay bills.
- Begin your scheduled bill paying and reconciliation.

STEP 2: GOAL SETTING

The difference between a wish and a goal is a plan. You can achieve any goal you want, no matter how wild it seems at first. If a goal is high (I'd like to be a multimillionaire), you can still reach it. It just means that the plan is more complicated, more difficult to execute, or longer range. Most likely it's the difficulty of the plan, not the enormity of the dream, that's the problem. Yet rarely do couples ever actually sit down to plan. They're more likely to express their desires as unfulfilled wishes than as more positive, defined goals.

Partners with the base problem of Conflicting Priorities will have different goals; that's the essence of the problem. In order to make your goals meet, you will have to use all the methods of conflict resolution (particularly taking turns) that we discussed. Before you can even begin, you must complete your goal-setting exercises. Partners who think their goals are similar and synchronized should take the goal tests together. Partners who find that their goals do not match should take the tests separately and compare them.

Goal Exercises

PART 1

On a scale of 0 to 5, circle the number to the right of each of the items below that most accurately reflects your financial concerns. A 5 signifies a priority item and a 0 indicates that that particular topic holds very little or no importance for you.

A. Current financial situation: do you wish to . . .

- Improve your present standard of living?   0 1 2 3 4 5

- Increase your net worth?   0 1 2 3 4 5

- Increase available disposable income?   0 1 2 3 4 5

- Provide a hedge against inflation?   0 1 2 3 4 5

- Provide funds for a significant capital expenditure (e.g., vacation home, school)?   0 1 2 3 4 5

B. Education Fund (If you have dependents): would you rather . . .

- Accumulate the total cash amount for your children?   0 1 2 3 4 5

- Or provide a set portion of that amount (i.e., one third or one half)?   0 1 2 3 4 5

C. Tax reduction/deferral   0 1 2 3 4 5

133

D. Investment portfolio: which of these describes
   your preferences?

   • Liquidity   0 1 2 3 4 5

   • Safety of principal   0 1 2 3 4 5

   • Present income   0 1 2 3 4 5

   • Long-term growth   0 1 2 3 4 5

   • Tax benefits   0 1 2 3 4 5

E. Invest in your own business   0 1 2 3 4 5

F. Retirement income:

   • Do you wish to maintain your present standard
   of living?   0 1 2 3 4 5

   • Do you anticipate a change in your lifestyle
   (e.g., more travel)?   0 1 2 3 4 5

   • Do you plan to sell existing assets to fund
   retirement?   0 1 2 3 4 5

G. Providing for dependents:

   • Do you wish to provide a guaranteed income
   in the event of your death?   0 1 2 3 4 5

   • Do you wish to provide a guaranteed income
   in case you become disabled?   0 1 2 3 4 5

   • Do you wish to preserve your assets in the
   event of a disability?   0 1 2 3 4 5

H. Charitable bequests:

   • Do you want to provide tax-favored bequests
   to the charity of your choice?   0 1 2 3 4 5

   • If so, would you do so now?   0 1 2 3 4 5

   • Or would you make such bequests from your
   estate?   0 1 2 3 4 5

The questions you have just asked yourself come with some modifications from New England Mutual Life's "Financial Goals and Objectives" questionnaire. These are the data that the financial planner finds most important in helping the client manage money. Now that you have taken the quick goal test, give it to the other decision-maker in your family and see if your goals are compatible. Where they are not, discuss why you disagree and find solutions by doing the goal exercise below. If you yourself are in conflict regarding goals, it will help if you do the following exercise as well.

PART 2

Answer the following in writing:
The best thing I ever did with my money is _____

because _____.

The worst thing I ever did with my money is _____

because _____.

PART 3

Now arrange your goals in the order shown in the example below:

Goals in Order of Priority	Date You Wish to Achieve Your Goals	Long Term/ Short Term	How Much You Will Need to Achieve Your Goal
Retirement	In 17 years	LT	$900,000 in tax-deferred retirement plan
Child's education	In 8 years	LT	$135,000
More life insurance	Immediately	ST	$2,000 premium per year
Acquire vacation home	In 2 years	ST	$42,000 down payment
Pay $10,000 in credit card debt	Over 2 years	ST	$13,400 principal and interest

Once you have clearly stated your goals, isolate those on which you agree and which can be reached most easily. Make a plan to achieve those goals, and go to it! Nothing succeeds like success. If you have arrived at a goal (no matter how small) that you both wish to fulfill (e.g., putting away $100 a month to fund an IRA), implement it immediately. Do not minimize the goals that seem easy to you. More people make that error than any other. The more goals you meet, the more goals you will meet.

Next, attack the goals that are tough. Do this by picking them apart, analyzing their components, and then making a plan.

For example, every family has its own list of important financial goals that can be achieved through budgeting. What are yours? Would you like to get yourself out of debt? Save for a home? Build your investment portfolio? Take your spouse and your kids for a two-week vacation at Disney World? Start a college fund for your children? Whatever your goal or goals, budgeting will help you realize them.

The budgeting procedure outlined in Step 4 is comparatively easy to understand and use. Not only will it help you take stock of your current financial situation, but it will also enable you to achieve the financial goals you've set for yourself and your family.

Step 2: Goal Setting Task Synopsis

- Set goals by completing exercises.
- Prioritize goals by completing exercises.
- Rewrite goals to make a five-year plan.
- Isolate and reach easy goals.
- Use conflict resolution to gain accord for goals that cause disagreement.
- Write plan to achieve more difficult goals.

STEP 3: DETERMINING CASH FLOW

Perhaps the simplest and greatest contribution you can make toward your financial well-being is to create a cash flow calendar. By this I mean a typical year-long calendar in which you first indicate with a blue pencil (OK, you can use red if you prefer) the times during the year when you expect a significant *outflow* (spending) of money.

By significant, I mean an amount that you find hard to accumulate quickly, an amount that you could not afford to pay on a regular basis. Of course, the meaning of the word *significant* will vary from couple to couple. For most couples, a significant amount is around $5,000 or less. For some couples this amount may be $250 to $500—for example, tuition payments in September, Christmas gifts in December, tax payments in April.

Now choose a different color pencil to mark those times that you expect an *influx* of money. Yellow markings may show a tax refund that you expect to get in July, a bonus in November, deferred compensation payments in January.

This gives you a yearly review of when large amounts of money will be coming in and large amounts must go out. You will notice that they don't usually coincide. This problem throws people off in their budgeting and financial planning.

Nevertheless, many of you will come out more or less even over the course of the year. The cash flow calendar works hand in hand with the Pay Yourself First Budget found in Step 4 to keep the budgeting dynamic and to keep you from getting into a money bottleneck during special times of the year.

The calendar was created by me for my clients who are successful writers, musicians, and negligence attorneys. What do these three professions have in common? They all have erratic income! In other words, they never know when their next dollar is coming in, although they know where it's coming from. Although their bills are steady, their income isn't. In order for them to plan financially, it's essential for them to create a calendar so that they can be sure of how to proceed.

For example, Jane and John receive a $12,000 tax refund in June. They go into a tizzy arguing over investment decisions. Because of her conservatism, they put it temporarily into a low-paying bank account or money market fund. He spends three months feeling guilty because he's "not doing anything" with his money. They interview financial planners, talk to their friends, and listen to financial gossip at cocktail parties. Finally, in the fifth month, in utter frustration, they put half into a six-month CD and the other half into a penny stock that is supposed to make a mint. One month later the yearly premium on his disability insurance is due, as are the land taxes on their home. All of a sudden they have no money. They sell the penny stock at a loss, take a penalty on the certificate of deposit, pay the bills, and declare themselves financially hopeless.

The problem is not poverty, it's cash flow. They should have been prepared for the real estate tax and disability payments. It's something they knew in advance and should have marked on the calendar. Had they seen this clearly, the $12,000 would not have been theirs to invest (and fight over). They should have placed the amount needed for definite expenditures in a six-month certificate of deposit that would mature at the time the money was needed. Although this is merely a method of "parking" money for a while, it is just right for such a situation. They would earn interest, take no risk in principal, and keep the money handy.

More fights take place over cash flow than budgeting. Budgeting is a matter of prioritizing, as you will see. Many couples are in accord with regard to their budgeting. What they fight about is deviation from the budget. This causes a feeling of lack of prosperity, a fear that clutches them when they can't make their payments, both fixed and flexible. This may not be because they don't have the money. It may simply be because they don't focus on when payments are needed and how much.

The cash flow calendar is a simple thing to draw up in the boardroom. It's more arts and crafts than it is financial planning.

For those with more serious cash flow problems, a weekly cash flow calendar can be prepared. After you have done your expenditure statement and your income statement, break these down to weekly income and outgo. Write this down on your calendar. For most weeks, income and outgo will be the same. For some weeks, however, you will see that small differences occur. Perhaps overtime payments are expected in one particular check, making your income slightly more in some weeks than in others. If you've worked at your job for a while, you'll know when those busy times occur. Conversely, some weeks you'll be able to predict high expenditures. You can even plan for them; if you have to shop for children's school clothing, you can make the date with yourself on your cash flow calendar. If you are going on vacation, you note when money will go out more rapidly than usual.

All the fights about spending too much (or spending injudiciously) that result not from the gross spending but from the *timing* at which expenditures take place are solved. So too is the issue of paying late charges on bills, which can cost a bundle at the end of the year if you are out of financial control. Even your filing system is geared to force you to pay those bills that will incur a penalty or service charge first. By jotting them down in your cash flow calendar, you'll be paying bills in the correct and most economical order.

If you find that your cash flow is *positive*, it means that by year's end you will have more money than you will have had to spend. This means you will have money to invest. And for those decisions you need to look at Step 6.

If you find that your cash flow is *negative*, this means that you will have spent more money than you have coming in by the end of the year. If you allow this to happen over a long period of time, you get deeper and deeper into debt that you cannot pay back.

Those who like to plan in great detail should also prepare the following *monthly* cash flow statement. You may use it only once in a while in "tough months" when you believe precision planning will help you avoid cash flow jam-up.

ESTIMATE OF MONTHLY CASH FLOW

For _____

As of (date) _____

SECTION 1. INCOME

Take-home pay _____

Bonuses, gifts, etc. _____

Interest _____

Dividends _____

Other income _____

TOTAL INCOME _____

SECTION 2. EXPENSES

Fixed Expenses

Rent or mortgage _____

Loan payments _____

Insurance premiums _____

Property taxes _____

Income taxes _____

Other taxes _____

TOTAL FIXED EXPENSES _____

Savings and Investments

IRA contribution _____

Other sav./invest. _____

TOTAL SAV. & INVEST. _____

Variable Expenses

Home furnishings	_____
Maintenance/repairs	_____
Home services	_____
Utilities	_____
Groceries, etc.	_____
Eating out	_____
Clothing	_____
Transportation	_____
Health care	_____
Education/child care	_____
Recreation	_____
Gifts	_____
Personal	_____
Pocket money	_____
Other	_____
TOTAL VARIABLE EXP.	_____
TOTAL EXPENSES	_____

SECTION 3. SUMMARY

TOTAL INCOME	_____
TOTAL EXPENSES	MINUS (−) _____
NET CASH SURPLUS	_____

Cash Handling

Part of effective cash flow management and budgeting is determining who handles the money and for what purpose. When there is a problem of Inequality, such as in the Beer and Bread Syndrome, where the breadwinner takes money for himself and leaves the rest for his spouse to manage the household, it is both (1) the amount he leaves her and (2) the fact that she must handle all the tasks that can cause trouble. This is particularly so if the Ralph Kramden Syndrome sets in, and he takes too little money for himself. If she says no to him when he asks for money, or if she has already spent the money on the household, the balance of power shifts to her, causing an imbalance in the relationship and a fight. Or an irate Kramden may accuse his wife of spending too much on the house and end up victimizing her. This happens too when one party uses credit cards without telling the other and without confirming the ability of the couple to pay the bills.

There are three types of money: cash, checks, and credit cards. *These are all vehicles for spending.* The problem with the credit card is that it doesn't feel like real money (sort of like the plastic chips you bet with in Las Vegas), and so we tend to feel less restricted in its use. A couple must work on who is *in charge* to avoid fighting (and becoming overdrawn at the bank!).

Select one board meeting for task allocations of this nature. Who will pay all the household bills? When a paycheck comes in, how will the money be divided? Will the earner take a percentage for their own spending money, will the rest be placed in a joint account for joint bill-paying? Will some be placed in an autonomous account for the nonearning spouse? (Such decisions can be made for large amounts of money, such as bonuses, as well.) In the chapter on task allocation, we saw that convenience is the major determining factor. If the wife does the shopping, she should handle the shopping money. If the husband pays the insurance bills, car payments, and garage rental, that money should be left in an account handy to him. If money is earmarked for investment, it should go either into a money market fund, where it may be drawn on readily for more lucrative investment, or directly to the checking account, to the broker, etc.

You may find that the wrong person is currently handling the money. The telltale signs of this occur when things are simply not getting done, bills are being paid late, and the couple always feels a little short. Which of you is the most efficient money manager? Don't guess—the two of you know who is best at it. Review your diaries to see whether money handling is at the core of your fights. Often couples confuse cash-handling problems with budgeting problems.

John and Nancy's diary showed several fights regarding her overspending. On one occasion John was furious when his credit card was turned down as he volunteered to pay for a business lunch. Nancy had used up the line on what he called a "shopping spree." On another occasion John refrained from buying a great new coat for himself because he couldn't be sure that Nancy hadn't "abused" the checking account again. The problem wasn't budgeting or lack of money. It was bad cash and credit handling. The cure was a good communication system in which Nancy *regularly* informed John of her expenditures.

The final phase of successful joint money-handling is reconciliation. This means a boardroom meeting at which the two of you reconcile what you have spent over the course of a month. Some of you may like to hold these meetings more frequently and others less. Use your communications bulletin board.

Step 3: Determining Cash Flow Task Synopsis

- Purchase a yearly calendar.
- Make dates of expected inflow and outflow of sums over $500 (or whatever sum feels significant to you).
- Determine who will pay bills.

- Fill out monthly cash flow sheets.
- Determine mode of communicating checking account and credit expenditures.

STEP 4: BUDGETING

With budgeting you are really in the thick of things in terms of both financial planning and disagreements over money. Disagreements, of course, arise when people have to prioritize. Because money is finite, something has to give. If your fights revolve over spending too much (as in the Lolita Syndrome, where she spends wildly and he's the beast of burden), budgeting together can actually save the relationship.

The process I recommend to couples to alleviate problems in budgeting is called the Pay Yourself First Budget. It is not so much a method of depriving yourself, or tightening your belt, as it is one of prioritizing your expenditures so that you make a monthly payment to your own regularly kept investment account. The "extra" money to pay yourself first comes from cutting those expenditures you rate as unimportant to you. In my previous book, *Your Wealth Building Years,* I gave youngsters a pep talk on the value of budgeting. It remains true for everyone, regardless of age.

I know that most of you rejoice if your expenditures equal your income. How will I get you to cut down even further in order to save/invest?—By giving you a new view of budgeting, spending, and investing. Like dieting, budgeting only works for the short term if it means deprivation. You cannot go against the grain; you cannot delay satisfaction (buying that painting, taking that trip, or purchasing that Italian suit) for too long before it all seems worthless. At least I can't. So let's forget the ugly defeatist word budget. Yuck! What I want has nothing to do with budgeting; let's call it repositioning. I want you to 1) know what you spend; 2) know how you allocate your income in terms of percentages; 3) prioritize your spending in terms of satisfaction; and 4) reposition your low-priority expenditures toward investments.

Before you get into the fray of prioritizing, sneak into it with a dispassionate approach to the true figures. To do this don't focus on how *much* money you spend, concentrate only on the *percentage* of your expendable income used for each type of expenditure. When this exercise is complete, you will have a picture of your spending habits that looks like the pie diagram you may have studied in economics class. To calculate the percentage that you spend on various items, fill out the quick income and expense statement on page 201–202. It will set out in round numbers, without requiring you to search through your data, how much you spend on the most significant items. It will also give you a quick look at your total income.

To make your pie diagram, use the figures from your quick income expenditure chart and divide by the individual expenditure. For example, if Sally and Karl earned $30,000 per year and spend $5,000 on food, then 1/6 or 18% of their budget is spent on food.

You may be shocked by the results of this exercise. You may find, as is true in the Kids vs. Us Syndrome, that expenditures are disproportionately high for the children and low for you and your partner. Or you may find that you are underspending with regard to shelter. Perhaps you will find that you're investing a greater proportion of your income than you think.

Take the case of Clara and Tom, who are wealthy by anybody's standards. They receive close to $200,000 in income yearly from Tom's family's trust fund. They came to my office for some important real estate investment planning. In the course of getting to know them, I learned that, surprisingly, they had fights over expenditures. They both felt like spendthrifts and were particularly guilty because they didn't actually earn any of the money they had. In fact, these were nice, down-to-earth, lucky people who were handed financial freedom and for the most part knew how to use it sensibly.

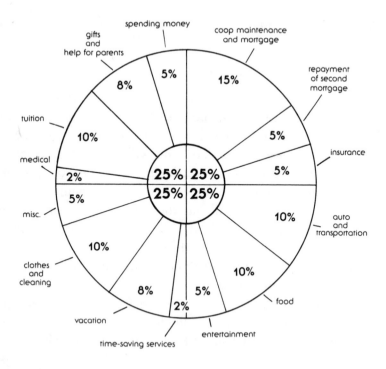

Nevertheless, as I gained their confidence, I found that they were a little scared. Money seemed to be flying out of their hands, and their lack of control bothered them, even though they had the wonderful security of a trust fund behind them. Just for fun, I asked them to do a pie diagram budget. They were absolutely amazed at what they saw. Of all things, they spent 20 percent of their budget on cars. They had two cars, both of which they kept in the city of New York, both of which were large luxury cars for which their garage charged them extra because of the liability and because each car took up a space and a half. They also had insurance, repair, and tuneups. What was even more remarkable was that they hardly ever used the cars.

Because they were wealthy people with lots of expenditures

and complex financial affairs, the issue of these cars never really entered their minds. They just saw a whole lot of money being spent inexplicably. They got rid of the cars and began a program of focusing more on what they were spending.

This is a happy story, because the people had no survival financial pressure. But it happens to everybody who does a Pay Yourself First Budget. There won't be one of you that doesn't find something silly, unnecessary, or of a low priority that you currently spend your money on. It should be fairly easy to find at least one item that you could eliminate and reposition as a saving or investment sum. This alone gives the feeling of working together and gets you on the road to success.

When you start to budget, be specific. Prepare a verified expenditure list. Now that you have a great filing system, you can use your check stubs or credit card receipts, or keep a record of your cash expenditures over a three-month period. Include all your expenditures. Don't kid yourself. If you add to your expense account without reimbursement from your job, don't delude yourself into omitting this as an expenditure.

Here is a sample list of typical expenditures.

Budgeting problems can be an expression of one or more fighting patterns. Any of the syndromes that concern Conflicting Priorities will be aggravated by the process of budgeting. Some of the Inequality syndromes are at the root of budgeting problems; often the Failure to Communicate syndromes will be highlighted. If you have great difficulty making your budget, here are some surefire tricks.

- Do not discuss anything about budgets outside the boardroom.
- When budgeting in the boardroom, use a pencil and paper and write things down.
- Do not discuss other matters in the boardroom, such as he or she not earning enough, being a failure, or comparing a more successful relative.

147

Expenses	Fixed Expenses	Flexible Expenses	Percentage of Spendable Income
SHELTER COSTS: Rent, heat, telephone, mortgage, electricity, maintenance, other utilities, taxes, snow removal, sanitation, gardening, swimming pool, other.			
SERVICES: Hair dressing, dry cleaning, transportation, professionals, tips, domestic help.			
FUN: Sports, entertainment, vacations, health club, country club, books, newspapers, pocket money, courses.			
DEBTS: Interest on personal loan, interest on credit card, other.			
NECESSITIES: Food, clothing, medical, pharmaceuticals.			
TAXES: Federal, state, local, gift, FICA/Social Security.			
INSURANCE: Disability, life, health, auto, home.			
CHILD RELATED EXPENSES: Education, child care.			
RELIGION & CHARITIES: Dues, contribution, literature, tithe.			
PAY YOURSELF FIRST: Investment, savings, pension/profit sharing, and other retirement planning.			

- Do not rehash old expenditures, like her extravagant coat or his boat.
- Do not discuss long-term goals yet, such as how you will obtain $100,000 to pay for the kids' education.
- Just do the numbers without comment. Don't whistle, as in "Whoooo, I never realized you spent so much on clothes!" If things get tense in the boardroom over budgeting, prepare your figures before you enter, have one or both of you go through checks, and present the figures in a report with substantiation.
- Keep a small pocket diary. This will help you keep a weekly cash record for money you spend on taxis and other cash purchases.
- Try to save as many check stubs and receipts as you can. This will give you a good record of expenditures.

Fixed or Flexible Expenses

Once you have prepared a present budget, categorize each expense as fixed or flexible. You have discretion over the latter but not the former. Loans and shelter are the two most common fixed expenses. Can any others be reduced without pain? Even with fixed expenses, ask:

- If the expense is a loan payment—Should I refinance for a longer period at lower interest to reduce expenditures?
- If the expense is in shelter costs—Have I gone overboard in choosing my digs? (Shelter is usually calculated as 33 percent of spendable income in urban areas, and 25 percent elsewhere.)

Usually it is the flexible expenses that devour earnings. Prioritize. Simply rank your expenditures as important, moderately important, and unimportant. Begin by eliminating the unimportant items. This in itself may be enough to begin a savings/investment plan satisfying to you. If not, eliminate some of the moderately

149

important expenditures. Then Pay Yourself First! Don't just eliminate the amount, write out a check to a special account and start
saving. The kind of account depends on how much you have. If
you begin with $50 it must be a savings account; if you are retire-
ment-minded, use an IRA until $2,000, the maximum contribu-
tion in any given year, is completed; if you have more available,
invest in a money market fund or begin to purchase units in a
mutual fund.

If necessary, send yourself a bill to pay yourself first. Place the
bill in your filing system under "Unpaid Bills—Penalty." Make
yourself as important as your creditors. You'll be amazed at how
regularly you will be able to save and how the savings will soon
become investments.

Tips for Budget Prioritizing

• *What appears to be a fixed expense may be flexible.*   It is not
a mark of failure if you have to move because you chose too high
a rental apartment in the first place; it's a mark of good judgment.
• *Don't give up wanting an item if you can't purchase it now;
simply change the date of purchase.*   Frequently an item can be
obtained but just not immediately. It can help couples who suffer
from the Now vs. Later Syndrome if the partner who wants a
particular item knows he or she will get it in three months, a
year, etc. If you have an "end" in sight you often can get a consensus.
• *Don't concentrate on who spends money on what.*   Many
budgets are foiled by the fact that one partner or the other is
expected to spend their money on certain items. For example, for
years women who worked were expected to use their money *for
extras,* such as vacationing, entertainment, and clothing, or the
kids' education. The husband, on the other hand, used his money
for *essential support*—rent or mortgage, medical bills, etc. This
kept the wife feeling that her money and her work wasn't quite
so important, and left the husband buckling under the pressure

of the major financial responsibilities. Don't allocate who will spend for what while budgeting. That's not the issue and can only bring up feelings of inequality at this stage. You should already have dealt with the task of handling cash flow. For those of you with serious problems of Conflicting Priorities or Inequality, a number of compromises will be necessary. Keep a compromise list and review it in two months. See if the picky nature of the demands have lessened. See if there's a better sense of fair dealing in spending. You'll be surprised at how, over time, you will begin to work in concert.

For those of you working alone, the only answer is to prepare the budgets and prioritize yourself. However, since you have another living, breathing human being to deal with eventually, a boardroom report or presentation must be made. *You* can create the boardroom atmosphere. Make an impressive presentation. Think of it as a job interview or a meeting with a loan officer of a bank. You may be angry with your partner because he is not participating, but you want him to take action, so you must do a planning job. Show the budget sheets, show the prioritizing that you've done. Show the cash flow calendar and show the decisions you've made based on them. It is difficult in the face of such a formidable presentation for your mate to ignore your plan.

If you cannot get your mate to sit down and listen to such a presentation at a boardroom meeting, there is likely a serious inequality in the relationship. Relationship counseling may be the next step. However, don't jump to conclusions. These techniques take time. You may be surprised to find that two weeks after your presentation your money-mate will say, "Could I see those papers again that you showed me last week?"

How Budgeting Can Change Your Lifestyle

Intensive budgeting *can* help couples change their life style. Take the case of Kelly and Harmon, who had dreams that seemed to tug at them wherever they went. She wanted to write a novel, he wanted to compose a symphony. They had resisted these dreams through nine years of marriage. Yet everything they did allowed them to keep the options open to follow these dreams. For example, they didn't have any children; they didn't buy a home; they took low-pressure jobs that didn't pay much. It seemed they were saving themselves for something, that one day there would be an explosion of creativity and they would give birth to their novel or symphony. Unfortunately neither ever did. They always felt too poor to quit even their low-paying jobs. They also felt that their marriage would be jeopardized if one got their wish and the other didn't.

I never would have seen them had Kelly not received a small bonus ($6,000) and come to my office for advice on investing it. I met them later on again in one of my seminars, which we offer to all our investors. I liked them both because I saw a spark of idealism that I hadn't seen for a long time. I offered to help them out through discussions. It turned out that what they needed was a Pay Yourself First Budget. They made the budget and together we *prioritized* to fit their dreams in. It turned out that Harmon felt he could write his symphony if he worked part time and had a break from work of three or four years. Kelly needed a solid year to write her novel. Moreover, she wanted that year to be at the site of her novel, in Spain, away from Harmon and away from having to earn any money. Don't think that this couple did not fight over these priorities; they did. It took four months of them working together in a boardroom atmosphere and six one-hour consultations in my office to get the matter straight.

First we determined every expenditure they made, plus an alternative budget for one year for Kelly abroad. Because they were not high earners we did this almost to the penny; the couple called pensiones, travel agents, and apartment exchange services to find out the price of living abroad. I reviewed the couple's lease to see if it was worthwhile for him to live at home during the year they would not be living together. We also geared up to increase their income by having them work for one full year and take advantage of certain overtime possibilities that they had been avoiding because they did not want to be caught up in the "rat race." We also prioritized dates. Kelly was to get her year immediately. Since Herman needed three or four years, he would use the first while she was away and then get two more when she came back. The couple on their own even budgeted long distance phone calls between the two of them on a very frequent basis and three visits home during the year from Kelly. It became increasingly clear that this couple wanted to stay together. They wanted to do their creating in the framework of their relationship.

The budget was made and set. At the present writing, Kelly is in Spain working on her novel and Harmon has taken on six students in addition to his usual job. If their works of art turn out to be as creative as their budgeting, they'll have a *magnum opus*.

The Time/Money Balance Sheet

If you find that cutting down on spending is just not resulting in enough saving, I suggest you do a second listing of expenditures you make in order to save time. Many young people in a hurry spend a small fortune on time-saving services. Prepare a Time/Money balance sheet, which puts you in control of the money you spend in this way. Use it:

- To help you spend less money by eliminating services that do not save you time.
- To help you reduce anxiety about spending for services that do not save you time.
- To help you judge what you should charge for your services.
- To help you judge the value of others' services to you.

In Column A, list the activities you hire others to do for you. Our hypothetical couple's list includes restaurants, dry cleaners, gardening, taxis, directory assistance, accounting, house cleaning, haircutting, and more.

153

Activity	Cost Per Week	Time Saved P/W	Money/Time Ratio	Comments
Hair cutting	$10.00	3 hours	$3.30	
Eating out	$35.00	1 hour	$35.00	
House cleaning	$40.00	5 hours	$8.00	
Dry cleaning	$10.00	2 hours	$5.00	
Lawn mowing	$1.00	10 min. (.1 hr)	$6.00	
Gardening	$3.00	20 min. (.2 hr)	$9.00	
Taxis	$12.00	3 hours	$4.00	
Home repairs	$20.00	3 hours	$6.00	
Snow removal (leaf cleanup)	$1.00	20 min. (.2 hr)	$3.00	
Wallpapering	$1.00	10 min. (.1 hr)	$6.00	
Directory assistance	$5.00	0	*	
Accounting services	$5.00	20 min. (.2 hr)	$15.00	

In Column B enter the money you spend per week for the service (if the expense is monthly or yearly, divide by 4.3 or 52 respectively).

In Column C enter the time per week you saved by paying for the service (do not fool yourself).

In Column D enter your Money/Time Ratio, the figure you get by dividing the money spent by the time saved.

In Column E comment on the result:

- Are you saving any time at all (e.g., when using directory assistance)?
- Is it a good deal, a cheap way to save time (e.g., a haircut)?
- Are you enjoying the service as well, and therefore would like to keep it up for other than time-saving reasons (e.g., eating out)?

Step 4: Budgeting Task Synopsis

- Create a pie diagram of your budget.
- Create a Pay Yourself First Budget.
- Prioritize flexible expenditures.
- Create a time/money budget.
- Set up an automatic Pay-Yourself-First account with a bank or mutual fund.

STEP 5: CALCULATING NET WORTH

Financial control does not mean never having to count your money! It does mean counting your money in terms other than the "bottom line." It is typical of Americans to dream of becoming millionaires, or to compare how *much* money they have today with how they were doing in the past. Thus "gross assets" becomes a measure of self-worth. This is inevitable in a society where much of life's values, fashions, styles, and social status is measured in dollar signs. Unfortunately, the measure of a husband or a wife can also be bound up with the "bottom line."

When a couple suffers from Dashed Expectations, then true net worth may be hard to face. If one mate (usually the husband) was expected to perform financially up to a certain level and has failed, there is often a great deal of hostility and tension surrounding the preparation of a net worth statement. While this is actually a very mechanical, dollars-and-cents exercise, it can cause a lot of trouble. Frequently, it's the spouse who didn't measure up to their *own* expectations who's ashamed and afraid to face their personal bottom line. Often, families who own their own business avoid net worth calculations because they don't want to calculate and quantify the value of that business. They are fearful it will reveal that the business (which they love and have nurtured) may not really be worth all that much.

Similarly, when there are syndromes relating to a Failure to Communicate, the preparation of net worth can be a problem, particularly if one or both of the team players had hidden assets.

Net worth preparation requires revealing the existence of assets and focusing on their present value. The secretive wife who has accumulated a nest egg may be ashamed or even afraid to reveal it. So too the husband who has felt powerful because of his control over financial information can get hostile or stubbornly uncooperative when forced to reveal information. In some cases the money-managing spouse feels their territory is being invaded or that their spouse's participation indicates that they have not been doing a good enough job. Let's look first at the importance of the graded net worth statement and then the methodology for preparing one. Later we can deal with the tough problems of overcoming the barriers created by fight-pattern syndromes.

The purpose of the graded net worth statement is to allow you to reposition your existing assets and replace them with different assets that better serve your investment goals. In addition, the graded net worth statement allows you to choose intelligently in the future in making new investments. Every investment has a purpose. Once you know your goals you will know the role your investment must play. Then you can apply the grading system described below to any investment available to you.

The Eleven Net Worth Grading Factors

You must grade your assets not just on their "bottom line value," but on their suitability for you as well, in terms of eleven different characteristics:

1. liquidity
2. cost
3. leverage
4. use as collateral
5. monitoring and expertise
6. income potential
7. growth potential
8. loss potential
9. volatility
10. inflation fighter
11. tax consequences

Every investment can be analyzed in terms of these eleven characteristics. Here's a quick rundown.

Liquidity means the speed at which one can sell an investment if cash is needed. Owning highly liquid investments (e.g., stocks) does not mean that you won't lose money. It means you can get your money out immediately with a phone call to your broker. On the other hand, real estate, which requires a good deal of searching for a market, is not a very liquid investment.

Cost concerns how much you have to spend to buy the investment. To some wealthy people, investments may be too cheap! For example, our office structures real estate investments for which $25,000 to $50,000 is needed per investor. My wealthier clients find that although the investments have good potential, they are too small; they would rather have one much larger investment.

On the other hand, a young couple with $2,000 to $3,000 to invest may not be able to afford such an asset. For them, a mutual fund that will accept $500 first purchases, then $100 a month, is a much more realistic investment.

Leverage and **collateral** are close relatives. Leverage merely means that you can use the asset itself as security to purchase it. The most highly leveraged investment is real estate. Usually a creditor like a bank or the seller will lend you 75% to 80% of what you need to purchase the asset by using it as its own security. This is called leverage. Collateral means that the asset is eligible *after* you own it to be used as security for a loan. If you already own a CD (certificate of deposit) and need the cash but do not want to withdraw it and incur a penalty, you might take a loan using the CD as collateral. Most banks will give you a loan of up to 90% of the value of your certificate of deposit. If you understand the collateral aspect of an investment, you may not be afraid to tie up your money. Many people stay out of investments because they feel they may need the liquidity. They don't count on the collateral feature of many securities.

Monitoring/expertise measures how much of your own time you have to devote to learning about and following an investment. To some people investing is a wonderful hobby. They already have an investment background. They love the experience of looking in *The Wall Street Journal* daily to see how their assets are doing. For others it's a drain on time and energy they could do without. Most high-risk investments, such as commodities, move up and down quickly and need a lot of monitoring; long-term bonds, on the other hand, need very little.

Income, growth, and **loss potential** reveal what you can gain from your investment and your chances of losing your principal or interest. Most guaranteed term investments are those with least risk, least monitoring, and least growth. Often, these are bank accounts, federal notes, bills, mortgages, and bonds where principal is guaranteed by the government. Loss potential is low. Usually, however, there will be little or no growth of your principal. What you hope to gain from such investments is a steady income. Compare these investments and grade them by how much income they yield.

A different sort of investment is one from which you expect growth. The more conservative of these investments have very low loss potential. An example of this would be blue chip stocks, which pay dividends and can appreciate in value slowly. Conservative investments in real estate in already proven locations is another example. The investment community often uses the phrase "No guts, no glory!" By this they mean that loss potential is usually proportionate to potential to appreciate.

When people come to a financial planner, they very rarely categorize themselves as risk takers. They don't want to lose their money. However, occasionally it's worth taking the chance of losing principal if you can afford it and the appreciation potential is very high. If you are new at investing, don't take risks. Wait awhile; you'll learn soon enough. Don't try to get rich quick. Not only will you lose your money, but you're likely to get cold feet about ever investing again.

We have all occasionally made a bet. When you involve yourself with penny stocks, or a company that you know very little about, you are doing nothing more than placing a bet. You are not making an investment. Every once in a while a bet can pay off, and you'll be happy with it. This is not, however, how people actually make money in the long run; it is how people get into fights.

Inflation fighter and **tax** aspects of investing vary almost yearly. How much tax you will pay if an investment is sold depends on your overall picture for that year as well as any new tax laws that may have cropped up while you weren't looking. Inflation varies from year to year. Regardless of whether or not you need an inflation fighter, it is important to reanalyze periodically.

An inflation fighter is simply an asset that goes up in value proportionately with rise in prices. The dollar you have invested in the asset will continue to buy more as prices rise. These investments are also popularly called "hedges against inflation." Gold is the perfect hedge against inflation, since it is currency and rises in value as prices inflate. Real estate is a good inflation fighter in most markets. Bonds—which, after all, are only evidence that you lent your money to a state or the federal government in return for a fixed interest rate—are among the worst. Because they are income-only investments, and fixed income at that, they tend to decrease in value as interest rates available from other investments go up.

Before you take another step toward the making of money, you must list the assets you already have and grade them in accordance with the eleven aspects of investments.

Preparing the Net Worth Statement

To see where you are at the moment, list all your assets in the following chart.

For this list the approximate date of acquisition is enough. The purpose is to see how long you have held the investment and focus on your situation at the time of the original purchase. What was suitable then may not be so now. If you decide to sell, don't blame yourselves for making a mistake; times have simply changed. To determine the after-tax value of an asset if it is sold, you must know the "basis." This means its purchase price plus the cost of improvements, if any, and sales costs (e.g., brokerage commissions, attorneys' fees, if any). Subtract this basis from the fair market value to ge the actual profit on which a tax will be calculated. If the fair market value is less than the basis, you have a loss, which may be deductible from your income tax. For the purposes of this chart an estimated value is sufficient. The annual growth of an *income* investment can be expressed in dollars per year and its yield (income) as a percentage of principal. I suggest both to help you easily compare investments with one another. If you have used the asset as collateral for a loan, you'll have to pay off the loan when you sell the asset. With this in mind, you can determine the actual cash you will derive from a sale, which in turn is available for a new investment.

INVENTORY OF ASSETS

Cash-Type

Items	No. of Units or Shares	Date Acquired	Amount, Cost, or Other Basis	Fair Market Value	Annual Yield		Collateralized?
					%	$	
Checking Accounts (mo. avg.)							
Savings Accounts							
Money Market Funds							
Treasury Bills and Notes							
Commercial Paper							
Certificates of Deposit							
Life Insurance (Accumulated Cash Surrender Value)							
Other (specify)							
Subtotal							

U.S. Govt., Municipal, Corporate Bonds, and Bond Funds: Issuer, Maturity, Call Dates

Subtotal							

Preferred Stock: Issuer, Maturity, Call Dates

Subtotal							

161

INVENTORY OF ASSETS (cont.)

Items	No. of Units or Shares	Date Acquired	Amount, Cost, or Other Basis	Fair Market Value	Annual Yield %	Annual Yield $	Collateralized?
Common Stock							
Subtotal							
Warrants and Options: Issuer, Expiration Date							
Subtotal							
Mutual Funds							
Subtotal							
Real Estate							
Residence							
Second Home							
Investment Real Estate							
Rental Residential							
Rental Commercial							
Time share							
Other (specify)							
Subtotal							

Miscellaneous Long-Term Assets   INVENTORY OF ASSETS (cont.)

Items	Date Acquired	Amount Cost, or Other Basis	Fair Market Value	Annual Yield		Collateralized?
				%	$	
Annuities						
Vested Pension/Retirement Benefits						
HR-10 Plan (KEOGH)						
Individual Retirement Acct. (IRA)						
Mortgages Owned						
Limited Partnership Units						
Patents, Copyrights, Royalties						
Receivables						
Other (specify)						
Subtotal						

Personal Assets

Household Furnishings						
Automobile(s)						
Recreational Vehicles						
Boats						
Jewelry/Furs						
Collections (art, coins, etc.)						
Other (specify)						
Subtotal						
Total Assets						

Grading Your Net Worth Statement

Now grade each investment that you already own on a scale of 1 to 10 with respect to how well it fits into your investment needs. To do this you must look again at the eleven characteristics of investments on page 157 and prioritize among them. What's more important to you right now, liquidity or growth? If you are expecting a change in your lifestyle, you may want liquidity. After all, if you tie your money up in a growth investment such as commercial real estate and you need the money soon to buy your own residence, you'll have to sell fast and cheap. If you're planning to have a child you are going to need income. No matter how good the growth potential of a long-term investment is, it will put you under undue pressure. You're just not ready to take advantage of growth investments. Therefore, a super-liquid investment such as a money market account or a relatively liquid investment such as a short-term CD or short-term bond is a better idea.

Your Retirement Net Worth Statement

Throughout the years of making net worth statements for couples, I have found the most useful single piece of advice is to separate long-term and short-term investments. In fact, you may want to make two separate sheets—one for long-term net worth and the other for short-term. If you have bought investments to meet long-term goals (e.g., unit trusts or bonds) or are holding assets in your pension plan, you may have difficulty evaluating them in today's market. You must judge your retirement plan as of your date of retirement, not as of today. Because of this I suggest that you make a separate future net worth statement for the picture you expect at retirement. List your pension income, Social Security, and long-term investments at future value. If you are satisfied, you've cinched your retirement. If you're not, use the next step, Investment Planning, to reposition your invest-ments and meet your goals.

Step 5: Calculating Net Worth Task Synopsis

- List your assets and pertinent information on net worth sheets.
- Prioritize according to the eleven different aspects of invest-ments.
- Grade your investments according to those priorities.

STEP 6: INVESTMENT PLANNING

There are many theories of investing, but none of them will work for you until you know first who you are financially.

Buying an investment is like buying any other product. You must know what you want before you shop. If you don't, one of two things will happen. Either you'll be so traumatized and con-fused that you'll buy nothing, or someone will sell you what they want you to buy. You must avoid both when it comes to making investments. The closer you are to knowing exactly what you want to buy, the better your decisions will be. If you know you want to buy a shirt, that's a step in the right direction. If you know that you need a blue shirt with a size 15 collar, long sleeves, and French cuffs, you are going to get precisely what you want, or you won't buy.

To figure out which investments make sense for you, evaluate the eleven characteristics described on p. 157, and explain your priorities to your broker. Almost any broker will be able to give you a potpourri of stocks, bonds, or other investment vehicles that fit your picture.

Let's take a specific couple as an example. He is an executive earning $55,000 a year and she a part-time travel agent earning

$12,000 a year. They are both fifty years old and have two children, one married, the other in college.

In looking at the eleven properties of investments, they have come to the following conclusions together: (1) they have sufficient liquidity (because the husband can borrow from his company under an employee benefit loan program) in the event of an emergency; (2) they prefer a leveraged or collateralized investment; (3) growth is very important to them since they have sufficient income; (4) they are in the 33% tax bracket; (5) the husband is very busy but the wife would like to involve herself more in monitoring investments; (6) they find they are both conservative when it comes to risk taking and do not really want to risk losing their principal despite their need for growth; and (7) they are not particularly afraid of inflation. (The amount of real estate they have and their gold fund is sufficient as hedges against inflation for their needs.)

Their long-term corporate bonds (totaling $50,000) should be repositioned (sold) because they merely give them unnecessary taxable income. They are ready to sell their bonds, since they grade very low. However, what are they ready to buy?

After analyzing the eleven characteristics of their investments, this couple knew pretty well what they were after. They wanted a nonliquid, $50,000 growth investment that could be used as collateral, require some monitoring, but was not necessarily a hedge against inflation, and carried only moderate risk. I suggested a well-balanced portfolio of emerging growth stocks (companies with an established record, but still growing in recession) in proven industries such as food and entertainment. Here there would be room for growth, the stock could be used as collateral for a low-interest broker's loan, and, in keeping with the couple's interest, only moderate monitoring would be required.

When a couple has a firm grasp on their financial needs, as this one did, they have taken a monumental step toward stopping the fight over money and making some. Much of the fear and insecurity that form the basis for money fights is gone. The partners are no longer innocents; they are adults with a concrete plan. This also means that if the investment does not meet their expectations, they have a framework of priorities that enables them to replace it with something different. They can diversify the investment as often as they like to meet as many as possible of the goals they are seeking.

You can see how some of the fighting syndromes are alleviated by the mere preparation of the graded net worth statement. Dashed Expectations can be the result of too little income. When money is investment for increased income, the bitterness caused by deprivation can sometimes be eliminated. Feelings of Inequality are diminished considerably when both parties have equal knowledge. Sometimes the secretiveness that lies behind a Failure to Communicate is also broken down by the mere preparation of the net worth statement. This is so for a very practical reason. When a couple is making decisions based on their total net worth and making each investment work for them, decisions will be inappropriate if one party has concealed significant assets. For example, if decisions are made on the basis of a need for liquidity when a $100,000 bearer bond has been stashed away, eventually this can hang heavy on the shoulders of the secretive mate. As I have reported in the past, secretiveness can be a red flag for a relationship in trouble. However, when secretiveness stems from a feeling of financial insecurity, the fear can be alleviated by financial planning.

Once you have made your commitment to gather data and have set goals and priorities, you will learn together how much you actually have to invest and the purposes your investments must serve. You will also have a mechanism to handle the changes in your priorities and fortunes. Let's say you have determined that you have a total of $100,000 in assets, including everything but your home. What should you do next? Make a pyramid chart.

As you identify the role your investments must play and implement your plans, you will find that you have amassed a diversified portfolio. Many financial planning manuals have pyramid charts to guide you. In my opinion a generic chart is unhelpful, but one you create in your own boardroom can do you a lot of good. Take a look at the two diagrams below for two different couples, the first in their thirties looking for growth through real estate and stocks, the second in their sixties looking for conservative income and a hedge against inflation

After making such a pyramid, your next and final investment step is to visit brokers and investigate several products. You must take time to educate yourself. Perhaps a fee-paid financial planner, who can show you how an investment is most likely to perform over the years, is a good idea. Such planners charge by the hour for their services ($50 to $150); the average plan costs somewhere between $300 and $2,500, depending on complexities and tax computations. Planners advertise or can be found by word of mouth. Some are CFPs (certified financial planners); others are brokers, lawyers, or accountants. A few planners have joined the Registry of Financial Planners, a nationwide directory of planners issued by the International Association of Financial Planners located at Placktree Plaza, Atlanta, Georgia.

If you are handy with a computer you may want to buy some of the software that helps you calculate returns over time, compound yields, and after-tax capital gains. Either way, the more you can foresee the results of your actions, the more likely you'll be to make investments.

Step 6: Investment Planning Task Synopsis

- Review your goals.
- Review your priorities with regard to the eleven characteristics of investments.
- Choose a financial planner or use computer software to make your own projections.
- Sell low-graded investments and replace with high-graded investments (reposition).

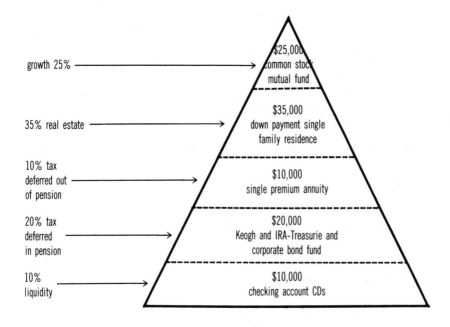

growth 25% → $25,000
common stock
mutual fund

35% real estate → $35,000
down payment single
family residence

10% tax
deferred out → $10,000
of pension single premium annuity

20% tax
deferred → $20,000
in pension Keogh and IRA-Treasurie and
corporate bond fund

10%
liquidity → $10,000
checking account CDs

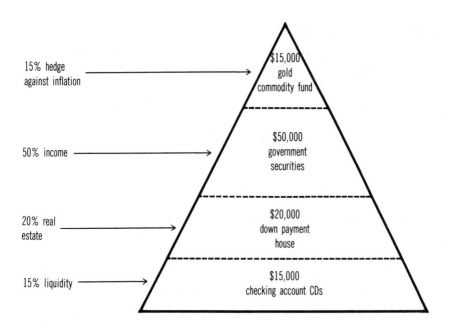

15% hedge
against inflation → $15,000
gold
commodity fund

50% income → $50,000
government
securities

20% real
estate → $20,000
down payment
house

15% liquidity → $15,000
checking account CDs

STEP 7: HANDLING CREDIT

The most controversial area of financial planning is the use of credit. Ours is a credit-oriented society. It's almost impossible to have a "commercial" identity without establishing credit. ("Let me see your credit card for identification, Mr. Smith. What? You have no credit card? Well, then, let me see your driver's license. What? You have no driver's license? I'm afraid, Mr. Smith, that you do not exist.")

It's no surprise, then, that fights over the use of credit cards are frequent. Budgeting is all mixed up with the payment of debts, fixed expenses, and the need for immediate gratification, which often leads to debt. Fights regarding debt are often a matter of temperament. In my book *Your Wealth Building Years*, I describe an insidious myth: that debt is always dangerous and that one should keep away from it at all times. This is simply wrong. The difference between someone who's going to do well and someone who's going to do brilliantly financially is the proper use of credit (the flip side of debt). Yet there are many people who so fear debt that they don't even buy their first home because of the pressure they will incur from the mortgage debt. When one teammate shuns debt and the other is willing to embrace it, fights occur.

There is no question that runaway debt can be disastrous. At its extreme, it leads to bankruptcy and affects a couple's credit rating for some time. Only after painstaking rehabilitation can creditworthiness be reestablished.

Many severe problems in a relationship occur when one party incurs debt without the knowledge of the other. If the debt is managed and paid, there's often no problem. If the team member gets behind in payments, the entire relationship can blow up.

If debt problems are so severe that your finances as a couple may really drag you under, there are some emergency relief organizations that can help you. The most prestigious one, located in New York City and run by Luther Gatling, is aptly named

BUCCS, which stands for Budget and Credit Counseling Services (115 East 23rd Street, New York, NY 10010; 212–677–3066). You may also wish to consider a home study course with audiotapes and written materials called "How to Improve Your Credit in the Next 90 Days: A Simple Six Step System" by Daniel K. Berman ($49.50), available by writing to Rex Communication, 150 5th Ave., New York, NY 10003.

Even if your credit problems are not severe enough to warrant contacting a credit counseling service, like most Americans you probably do not really understand the proper use of debt and credit. For many couples, overuse of credit is not the problem. It's the mistaken belief that debt is always dangerous that causes difficulty.

Using Leverage

Anyone who goes through the forms in this book—the Pay Yourself First Budget, the repositioning of assets—and learns how to use the section on the chemistry of investments will do well. But what will separate those who become wealthy from those who are merely "comfortable" will not be investment brilliance as much as it will be understanding and using credit to build wealth. And you do not need to know much about credit; what you need to do is make an attitude adjustment, a change in your way of thinking and in what you have been taught.

There is no virtue, none whatsoever (no matter what your mother told you), in using your own cash for investments. If you can get 100 percent financing on an investment, take it. Let's say you have saved $5,000 and would like to make an investment in real estate. Except for public limited partnerships, there probably is no investment you could possibly make. On the other hand, let's say someone has an apartment in co-op ownership worth $55,000. If they are willing to take your $5,000 as a down payment and transfer to you the ownership of their co-op with an agreement that you will pay them $50,000 slowly over time at a particular interest rate, this allows you to buy. So one fundamental purpose

171

of financing, particularly for the younger person, is to make up for the cash that they do not have.

Now take the same concept a step further. Let's say you had the $55,000, in cash, to pay for that co-op. If you paid for it in cash, you might be able to make a deal for a better price and pay perhaps, $50,000, saving $5,000 on the purchase price. If the co-op appreciated in value by 10 percent (a not unreasonable yearly appreciation, even in a modest location), it would be worth, and you could sell it for, $60,500 at the end of a year. If you paid cash, you would have made $10,500 on a $50,000 investment—in other words, a 21 percent increase on your money. However, if you had financing and used only $5,000 of your own cash, you would have made the same $10,500 on a $5,000 investment. In other words, you would have earned over 200 percent on your money. That's the importance of leveraging: the same investment, the same risks, and a startlingly different return.

The usual argument when people hear this example is that they can't afford to carry a loan for the remaining $50,000. If that is the case, then buy something cheaper that is leveraged. Use your Pay Yourself First Budget to learn what you really can afford. Let me give you some Dutch uncle advice: most people underestimate their ability to earn and to carry debt. If you cut out the 19 percent interest that you are paying on your credit cards, you will be able to carry a substantial amount of debt at 11 or 12 percent over the long term, for real estate or other types of investments.

Graded Liability Statement

As you have done with your assets, you should make a list of your liabilities. Once again, just listing what you owe is not enough, although it can be very therapeutic. You also must write down when the loan must be paid back, the monthly payments, the interest rates, whether the loan is collateralized, and any other interesting facts regarding your debt. For example, is there a balloon payment at the end that should be noted on your cash flow calendar? Are you paying interest only, or principal and interest, at each loan period? Does the interest rate vary so that there is a degree of uncertainty in your borrowing? Take a look at the following worksheet and use it to your best advantage in gathering the data regarding your debt.

Certain facts will emerge from your completed list. Compare the effective interest rates you are paying. Do you have cheap loans or expensive ones? Perhaps you should obtain a consolidation loan that will eliminate the more costly loans. Are some of your debts coming due more quickly than you expected? Use your cash flow calendar to put yourself back in control. Maybe now is the time for you to work on getting a refinancing so that you can extend the payback period. Will a major debt soon be paid? Will you be burning your mortgage, paying off your car entirely? If so, this debt that you have been carrying can turn into a Pay Yourself First investment program. Unfortunately, most people rejoice when they have made their last payment on a major debt and then go ahead and spend that money on consumables, never realizing that they've readjusted their spending to consume what used to be steady debt-service payments. Instead of doing this, rechannel debt service into investment or savings. All these things, including which of your assets have been useful as collateral, will become apparent merely by analyzing this chart.

Focus on What You Can Borrow

Now you must take step two: make a thoughtful list of avenues of credit that you have not tapped. Don't be afraid to do this. It does not mean that you have to use them or take a loan by any means. A listing of credit opportunities should be a joyful event. But be warned! It makes a lot of people nervous, particularly those who are insecure about their own ability to manage debt. They don't like to know how much is available to them because they are afraid they may use it. Interestingly, it is the more conservative teammate who is fearful of their ability to han-

INVENTORY OF LIABILITIES

Outstanding Obligations	Name of Creditor	Original Amount	Maximum Credit Available	Present Balance	Monthly/ Annual Repayment	Effective Interest Rate	Maturity Date	Secured Insured
Charge Accounts (stores)								
Charge Accounts (other)								
Credit Cards								
Short-Term Loans								
Personal Notes								
Family Loans								
Stock Margin Loans								
Life Insurance Policy Loans								
Income Tax Liability								
Federal								
State								
Local								
Property Taxes								
Investment Liabilities —limited partnership								
Mortgage(s)								
Liability Judgment								
Family Member Support Obligation(s)								
Child Support								
Alimony								
Other (specify)								
Total Liabilities								

dle debt. Because of this, they may blame the other team member for incurring too much debt. They may even be wary of learning what lines of credit are open to them for fear that the more aggressive credit user will become overextended. Think of the exercise as academic. Think of each credit line as a new asset. You could use it (spend it) or not. In the long run, people who feel rich and become rich do so because of the proper use of their credit opportunities. Of course, we will come back to the idea of *proper*. A helter-skelter approach to credit use is dangerous. That's not the purpose of this exercise. Answer the following questions:

Do you have hard assets such as coins, stamps, or art that are available to be pledged for credit?

Can you refinance any real estate, including your own residence, and if so, how much would the bank lend you?

Do you have stocks that have SMA (Surplus Margin Account)?

Do you have bonds or other nonpledged assets that can still be used as collateral?

Are student loans available to you?

Are personal loans available to you that are not collateralized?

Do you have borrowing power from your employer?

Do you have borrowing power against an insurance policy?

Do you have a credit card that gives you borrowing power?

Do you belong to an organization that extends loans (for example, The American Bar Association; my group has a $50,000 loan program for members)?

Do you have a business plan satisfactory to command a business loan from a bank or other institution?

Are you a member of a minority group or do you in other ways qualify for government loans?

Are there any other lines of credit that you have not yet tapped or considered?

Grading Your Credit Opportunities

Now you know what you have done with your lines of credit, and you also know what you have left undone with the use of your credit. Step three requires you and your teammate to analyze the most important aspects of credit use; this will send you far on your way to maximizing your credit opportunities. Always think of the use of credit and its flip side, debt, with regard to the following variables:

- Is the debt long term or short term?
- Is the debt cheap or expensive?
- Is the debt collateralized or not?
- Is the debt for investment or for consumables?

It's easy to see that all debts can be ranked or graded with respect to these four variables. For example, a debt that is long term, cheap, and not collateralized is the best possible debt to have. If you can get it, take it. There is even debt that's worth taking on even if you don't need it for anything! I won the United States Department of Labor Public Service Award in 1980 for teaching several hundred women in a special CETA Program how to borrow money from their own employers. The United States Government, which employed the women, was offering loans at 4 percent to its employees. At that time banks were paying approximately 6 percent on savings accounts. I taught the women how to make money on the float (the difference between the interest rate they were paying and the interest rate they were achieving). These women made very little money, and an extra 2 percent meant a lot to them. Moreover, the interest rates were tax deductible at that time, and while the women were in very low tax brackets, every penny helped.

By contrast, a short-term loan that requires immediate use of your cash flow at a high interest rate and that uses heavy collateral is only worth taking if you really need the money. Here is an example of my recent use of such a loan. The 1986 tax law caused many real estate owners to decide to sell their real estate before the close of the calendar year, so a capital gain could be taken for 1986 rather than waiting for a sale until 1987, when capital gain tax treatment would no longer be available. I was anxious to make a deal on a particular investment property and made a good one, provided I could close before the calendar year. After all my investment financing was complete and in place, I had an opportunity in the last week of the year to buy a second building adjacent to the first, which was very appealing to me. However, to secure that second piece of property, I had to pay $100,000 that I had planned to use to close on the first property. What should I do? Should I pass up the second piece of property, or should I have an enormous upheaval with my original seller and try to close in 1987? I went back and looked at my unused lines of credit.

I realized that in 1987 I was planning to close on a mortgage against a piece of country real estate. I already had a mortgage commitment and a closing date for the middle of January 1987. However, I needed the money now. Instead of going to a bank and asking for a personal loan based on the real estate I was going to buy, which would have caused a great deal of delay, I asked for a bridge loan to tide me over from the end of December 1986 to the middle of January 1987, when my mortgage closing would take place. I obtained a short-term loan against heavy collateral— my mortgage commitment. As soon as I got it, I had to pay off the bridge loan. Fortunately, the interest rate was not high (2 points above prime). Actually, it was lower than the mortgage I was eventually getting, which was, however, for a long term.

This teaches a consistent lesson. No loan is perfect. Each of the good points of a loan will be inversely proportional to the bad. For example, a short-term loan may have lower interest rates than a long-term loan. A noncollateralized loan will usually have higher interest rates than a collateralized loan. When you shop for a loan, you must prioritize what's most important to you. A cheap short-term loan is fine, provided you'll be able to pay it off in time. You might be happier with a more expensive loan that does not have to be paid for a long period. Remember also that interest and principal are often paid monthly. Sometimes the payment is for interest only. An interest-only loan is much cheaper to carry; however, you'll be left with a large balloon payment at the end, which must be accounted for in your cash flow planning.

Making Friends with a Bank

The average American couple is negligent in creating a relationship with a bank. Start immediately. First, try to get a personal loan from a bank. A noncollateralized personal consumer loan is the highest banking rate you'll find. Nevertheless, it is considerably lower than anything you'll get on a credit card, by a minimum of two points if not more. Next, should you already be in trouble with your credit cards, you might get what's called a consolidation loan: one loan from a bank that helps you pay off all your credit cards and reduces your interest rate. Most banks will give smaller consumer loans to a young person with a good steady job. If for some reason you can't get such a loan, your next step must be to get some money into that bank and open up a savings account. From that you will take a passbook loan for the amount of money that you have in the account. No bank will turn down a borrower who has an account with them if all they want to borrow is the same amount of money they already have in the account. They merely freeze the account, let it grow at whatever interest rate it is deposited at, and lend you the money to buy your items. Now you may ask, isn't it cheaper to use my cash, wipe out my account, and take no loan? Yes, it is cheaper, but not *smarter*. You need to develop credit, and this is the first step. Once you have established credit, you have also established your banking relationship (killing two financial birds with one stone).

Women's Credit Rights

On October 28, 1965, women achieved legal credit equality when the Equal Credit Opportunity Act took effect. The statute prohibited creditors from discriminating in any type of credit transaction on the basis of sex, as well as marital status, age, race, color, national origin, or receipt of income from public assistance (welfare). The statute also heralded the beginning of the Fair Credit

Billing Act, the Equal Credit Opportunity Act, the Fair Credit Reporting Act, and Consumer Leasing Acts.

For couples, this means quite a bit. Yet much of the public is still unaware of the existence of these acts. For example, many women do not know that:

- Women can now obtain credit in their own names.
- Single women will not lose their credit standing when they marry.
- Married women will not lose their credit rating when widowed or divorced.
- Alimony, child support, and separate maintenance must be considered as any other income.
- Mortgagers must consider a wife's income, part-time or otherwise, when evaluating a couple's creditworthiness.
- Creditors can't ask any questions regarding childbearing.
- Creditors must reveal their reasons for denying credit.

Many homemakers are concerned because they do not have their own independent credit rating and worry that they will not be able to get a loan in the event of divorce or widowhood. Others are concerned that their husband's bad credit habits will taint their own credit rating, spoiling all their years of diligently paying bills. These fears are legitimate only if you don't know your rights. For those of you who are not concerned with these issues, consider the following sad story. In 1974, I had completed two years of investigating the resale of individual condominiums in New Jersey. I was very interested in buying a few and getting my own financial portfolio started. I was married, a hardworking lawyer with a good income. Yet when my husband and I applied for a mortgage to acquire a rentable condominium (total price $33,000), we were turned down. It seems that the New Jersey bank refused to accept my salary, which was equal to my husband's, as part of our creditworthiness. Why? Because I was of childbearing age.

Eighteen months later my husband and I applied for our first mortgage to buy our own home. We were again turned down, for

179

the same reason. By this time our combined income was three times that of the national average. One bank after another refused us. Finally, a New York City bank gave us a loan based on a finding that, as an attorney, I could always work at home if I decided to have children.

The reality, of course, was quite different. I had no intention of working at home in the near future, whether I had a child or not. While both my husband and I were incensed by this belittlement of my career ambitions, we took the loan. Of course, it was the best thing we ever did from a personal finance point of view. However, I still pass by that high-rise condominium in New Jersey with one-bedroom apartments going for $175,000 and know that I could have cashed in on the situation had I been a man.

If I have such a story to tell, it is likely that almost every woman in America can cite an actual pocketbook loss resulting from credit discrimination. Well, we're mad as hell and we don't have to take it any more. At least not since 1965. Some salient features of the Equal Credit Opportunity Act are that childbearing practices cannot be inquired into; both full-time and part-time jobs must be considered; a wife's income may not be disregarded under the assumption that she will not return to work if she bears a child; and alimony, child support, and separate maintenance income must be considered.

For reprints of salient acts and statutes write to Federal Deposit Corporation, Public Information, 550 17th Street, Room 6061–B, N.W., Washington, DC 20429. Request:

- Fair Credit Reporting Act
- Equal Credit Opportunity and Women
- Equal Credit Opportunity and Age
- Truth-in-Lending
- Fair Credit Billing

Since throughout this book I suggest that separate accounts be kept between husband and wife or teammates in general, it is important to know that a woman's own creditworthiness can be used as the *sole* basis for opening an account or getting a loan. If you are creditworthy without the addition of your husband's resources, no lender can request information on your spouse's income or his credit history, nor can they require a co-signature, provided that you alone satisfy their credit requirements. This means should your spouse be *less* creditworthy than you, you may be able to get an independent loan.

The two of you together may feel discriminated against for reasons other than sex. The length of time you have stayed at a residence or worked at your job, and even possession of an account with the telephone company are all things the credit bureaus look at in making a quick credit report for you. Many credit institutions use this type of report to determine your creditworthiness. Naturally, they will also look at things you would expect, such as whether you have paid your bills on time. If you use my 10-Step Method, you'll have the type of filing system that protects your credit rating by forcing you to pay first the bills that incur late charges and penalties. These are usually the types of bills that are reflected first in a bad credit history. If you are beginning to re-establish good credit and you'd like to know what your credit rating is, you can pay for a copy of your credit history. You may request your credit file from any one of the 2,500 credit bureaus in the country. An example is TRW Credit Data. You can find these bureaus in the Yellow Pages.

Under the Fair Credit Reporting Act, you have the right to know what's in your file without any charge if it has resulted in your being turned down for credit in the last six months or for employment in the last two years.

If you've been frustrated by an incorrect bill, remember that, effective October 1976, the Fair Credit Billing Act makes it mandatory for creditors to resolve billing disputes, including disputed charges to your credit cards, within a certain period. If you receive a bill that in your opinion is incorrect, pay the amount you believe to be correct and write a letter to the company detailing your objections to the amount charged. You have sixty days after the bill was mailed to you to object. Within thirty days you must receive an acknowledgment of your letter; ninety days after this the company must send you either a corrected bill or an explanation of the disputed charges. If you are still not satisfied, write the Federal Deposit Insurance Corporation, Washington, DC 20429, if the problem is with a bank. Write the Federal Trade Commission, Washington, DC 20580, if the problem is with a loan or installment agreement.

Step 7: Handling Credit Task Synopsis

- Determine how comfortable you are about carrying debt.
- Grade your liabilities in terms of duration, cost, and collateral.
- Pay off low-graded debts and keep or increase high-graded debts.
- List unused credit opportunities.
- Establish a banking relationship.

STEP 8: INSURANCE

Insurance-related decisions are usually the easiest and least emotional to make. That doesn't mean that they are always correct. They are frequently made with little information or, worse, never made at all. The couple remains underinsured all their lives, leaving the dependent spouse in dire straits when the partner dies. In most cases, a previously adequate insurance policy is never reviewed as circumstances change, leaving many a young widow to learn that her husband's mother was the beneficiary of his only insurance policy.

Identify the Coverage You Have

Take an inventory of all of your present insurance. I realize this is as much fun as washing the kitchen floor by hand. But look at the bright side. The task is finite, and the reward is a feeling of solid security. The following charts require you to fill in the nature of the policies, the premiums you pay, the coverage you have, and the beneficiaries, owners, and insured. Life, medical, theft and casualty, auto, and disability insurance are all covered. After you have done this you'll see for the first time, perhaps, where you really are with respect to your insurance coverage.

LIFE INSURANCE

Legend: WH—Whole life   TM—Term   DI—Double indemnity life
       O—Other   EN—Endowment

Type of Insurance (use legend)	Company Name & Policy #	Beneficiary	Face Amount	Annual Premium	Options

MEDICAL INSURANCE

Legend: HO—Hospitalization   SU—Surgical   MD—Medical
       MM—Major medical   TR—Travel   ATR—Air travel
       DI—Disability   Accidental death   Accidental death
                     O—Other   MC—Medicare

Type of Insurance (use legend)	Company Name & Policy #	Persons Covered	Amount of Coverage (days in hospital; type of service; deductible)	Premium	Option

VEHICLE INSURANCE

Vehicle Insured	Company Name & Policy #	Amount of Coverage & Deductible	Insured Drivers	Premium	Option

DISABILITY INSURANCE

Disabilities Covered	Company Name & Policy #	Amount of Coverage & Number of Days Before Insurance Begins to Pay	Beneficiary	Premium	Option

Know What Your Policies Say

After you've done this, review the material on insurance options. Most of us have policies that we really don't understand. You may want to change some of the options you have already selected, or obtain those that you have failed to include. Your insurance agent will be more than delighted to help you.

Here are some options you are likely to run across.

Automatic premium loans. One useful option is to have the company use the cash value of a policy to pay premiums that you have forgotten to pay. This is a pretty good option to select, particularly if you are careless. If you are prone to leaving envelopes unopened, if you don't heed warnings, if you take long vacations or are slightly short of cash every once in a while, pick up this option; it's free.

"Paid-up" insurance. "Paid-up" insurance means that all the premiums you are required to pay from the time you take the policy to the time that you die (provided that you live to be 100 or less) are paid. It really is a prepayment program. People elect this because they fear that they will not have the money to make the payments after their retirement. They are worried about having fixed expenses when they are old. For most people, however, it's a bad idea. Unless you have done almost no planning in your lifetime, you will have less and less need for the policy as a death benefit as you grow older. If it should really happen that you can't afford to keep up your insurance, that will probably be in old age, the time when it is needed least, not most. Meanwhile, you will have been paying for very expensive insurance at the highest possible premium rates very early in life, when you need the money to build your estate. Once the policy is paid up, the interest accumulates with deadly slowness. Because of this there are few paid-up policies; the best thing to do with a paid-up policy is to cash it in and put the proceeds away in a certificate of deposit or treasury bill at the highest possible interest rates.

Retirement income policies. You should explore the single premium deferred annuities now on the market, particularly once your IRA or Keogh account is funded.

Modified life. For the person who wishes expensive straight life insurance but can't afford it, modified life insurance is both good and bad. A modified life policy permits you to pay a small amount of premiums; that's the good news. As years go on, however, you will be paying a disproportionately larger amount toward the end of the policy; that's the bad news. Actually, you're gambling on yourself becoming richer. Since I don't like a straight life policy, I'm not in favor of modified life insurance, either.

Disability waiver. With a disability waiver, for a small extra amount the company will continue making payments if you become disabled. This is usually a good option, because the key element is to make sure nothing happens that forces you to cancel your policy at a time when you would not wish to. Involuntary cancellation is the only real tragedy that takes place with respect to insurance. In investigating disability waivers, ask the salesperson at what age, if any, the disability coverage terminates, what the term disability itself means to the company, whether it matters how the disability arose (illness, accident, and so forth), and

185

how soon the disability is made payable (normally three to six months).

Double indemnity. For a small additional charge many companies will include a double indemnity clause in your policy. This means that your beneficiary receives more money if you die as the result of an accident than as the result of an illness. Why should your beneficiary get, want, or even deserve more money if you die accidentally instead of through natural causes? You will have provided for your family in precisely the same way, their needs will be exactly the same, the rest of your estate will be identical—and yet people are fascinated by this little gimmick called double indemnity. What it really means is that the insurance company gambles with you. Accidental deaths are actually quite infrequent. For a small extra amount, your family will get twice the death benefit if you should die in that fashion. If you feel it's worth a gamble and you enjoy that kind of thing, by all means go ahead. Make sure, though, that it's cheap thrill. Ask the salesperson exactly what the extra cost is.

A Matter of Priorities

Occasionally, fights develop over the purchase of insurance. Insurance must be looked at as a fixed expense. But its future orientation can cause aggravation of the Now vs. Later Syndrome.

If you find that you're fighting over the amount of insurance needed or the tasks relating to insurance, go back to basics. Use the Pay Yourself First Budget and prioritize the premium as a fixed expense. If you and your mate are at odds, you'll have to use the compromise techniques found in chapter 6.

Most people do not fight about insurance; they just don't know how much they need. To find out, try the following:

Prepare a needs budget for your family if you were gone. Put down what it actually costs your family to live. Include extraordinary expenses that will surely arise, such as a college education and repair of major equipment, if equipment is part of your everyday life (for example, farmers and their families).

Next, take the number of years you would like to provide for your family without their having to dip into other capital and without your spouse having to increase his or her earnings. At least ten years of financial security through insurance is usually appropriate. Take the yearly budget, multiply it by ten, add a 6 percent inflation factor, and add a one-time cost for education, equipment, or other extraordinary but expectable expenses. Subtract other income from all sources such as other investments, Social Security, and spouse's earnings. The result will give you a rough idea of how much of a nest egg you need to replace your earnings for a ten-year period.

Next, use a 10-percent-a-year return on investment and estimate how much increase you need. If you need an extra $10,000 a year for ten years over and above other resources to make up for your loss of earnings, then you buy $100,000 worth of insurance. At the end of ten years, only the income thrown off by this lump sum will have been used, and your family will be left with a tidy sum for continued investment. If emergencies have occurred through the decade, then at least they will have a fund to invade.

Your calculations might show that family needs are so great that it is impossible to pay for enough insurance to yield a satisfactory income. Take a second approach. Purchase enough insurance so that if the principal plus interest is divided by ten, and one tenth is used each year, the family could continue to live in the style to which they have been accustomed. Of course, at the end of the ten-year period no nest egg would be left. By then, however, the family would have made other adjustments for carrying on.

Once you have arrived at the amount you would like the family to have as a death benefit, do your shopping for the cheapest possible insurance.

Step 8: Insurance Task Synopsis

- Calculate your yearly contribution through earned income.
- Multiply by 10.
- Increase by a figure of no less than 4% per year for inflation.
- Seek out the least expensive term insurance to give you at least the death benefit in the amount you just calculated.

STEP 9: HOUSING

Because of the importance of housing decisions and the emotional component associated with them, housing must be isolated as a separate step. Those who are content with their present arrangement can skip to Step 10. But if housing is on your mind, read on.

It's Still Worthwhile to Buy Your Own Residence

Even though the tax laws have changed and the minuscule prices of the 1970s are gone, try if you can to buy your own residence. When residential real estate is held up to the light of the eleven characteristics of investments, it grades "outstanding"!

Why? Because real estate, properly chosen, generally increases in value, there is potential for growth and appreciation and little potential for loss. Residential real estate is probably the most easily leveraged investment. Mortgage money is always available if you know where to look. Further, real estate, once purchased, is a great source of collateral—for a second mortgage, for equity loans, for refinancing first mortgages.

Finally, the value of the real estate inevitably rises in inflationary times, largely because real estate is the one investment that is also a necessity. So why doesn't everyone run to buy real estate? If you listen to cocktail party chatter, you'd presume that they do! Everyone seems to own a co-op, condo, house, residential or commercial property, or all the above. Why not you?

Perhaps the answer is that without knowing the rules of investment analysis, you instinctively understood the difficulties of real estate purchase, especially for the younger investor. They are:

Cost. Even a 20 percent down payment can be out of reach; a mortgage may be too high a burden on cash flow; or tax savings and income don't equal the outlay.

Liquidity. If you must sell, it will take more than a phone call to do so.

Monitoring. Managing real estate can be a full-time job, and you don't have time.

Only if these above considerations present a severe problem should you choose to rent.

Many couples fight because one partner is dilatory about buying a house, perhaps even afraid to buy. A friend of mine relates how he and his family went to see houses every weekend for 10 years throughout his childhood and never bought. I call this real estate phobia.

To overcome this problem, the following steps must be taken:

Understand that there are many right choices. Real estate phobia stems in part from the incorrect belief that there is only one right house for you. People are so terribly confused about the differences between co-ops, condominiums, and houses that they cannot decide among them. They may also believe that it is financially shrewder to live either in the city or in the country, in a duplex or in a ranch house. They have the idea that if they could choose the precisely correct piece of property, they would make a million dollars. Under such decision-making pressure many people make no decision at all, and let each parcel of property go by the boards. There are wise decisions and poor decisions, but there is no single right decision.

Set priorities. You must establish your priorities and know *what you are willing to give up.* A good friend of mine and one of the most successful real estate speculators in the country pointed

189

out to me years ago that if I had a million dollars to spend I would have the same problem that I have with ten thousand or a hundred thousand; that is, I would have to give up something. Frequently I leaf through a magazine called *International Homes,* in which few of the homes pictured are under a quarter of a million and most are over a million. It's a wonderful education. I can actually look at a million-dollar house and say, "Gee, I don't like the shape of that swimming pool." The point here is that there is no perfect home; you will not find it for a million dollars and you will not find it for fifty thousand dollars.

Decide what you can afford the right way. Ultimately it is the money—the amount of it and the financing—that solidifies real estate phobia. "How much should I spend? How much should it cost?" become the operative questions. But there are no shoulds. In choosing a home, you must look at your personal budget to determine what you can spend. One misconception must be buried for all time: the idea that people show their wealth through the size and appearance of their home.

How Much House Can You Afford?

Make a readjusted budget before you buy and then stretch it. Check back to the Pay Yourself First Budget and create a fictional budget giving consideration to the items that come with home ownership (e.g., furniture, gardening, fuel, mortgage). Remember new transportation costs (will you need a car? will you save on train fare?). Rework this proposed budget several times *while* looking for property. Only a simultaneous combination of planning and looking will work. If your dream house is available, budget tightening *is* in order. Always buy a little better than you can afford.

Why? Because there is significant money to be made in residential real estate. All the books you can buy on "making a million on real estate," "pyramiding real estate," becoming "independently wealthy" with real estate are accurate.

If you can keep your first home (or your present house) and rent it to someone else instead of selling it when you want to move, you will make a lot of money. Most Americans are used to planning for the ever-increasing burden of home ownership. The scenario usually goes as follows: A young couple borrows from their family, adds their own savings, and buys small house. Their income, needs, and assets grow. They find a new, larger, more expensive home and scramble to sell their first home. Finally, after much trauma, they get a buyer. All appreciation and all their accumulated capital is put into the new, larger home. They are house-poor again. This happens twice or more until they retire, sell their last home, and wonder why they did it all in the first place!

However, if you can manage not to sell your first house, but to rent it when you move, you'll then enjoy the following scenario: A young couple buys their first home. Income grows, as does home value. They take an equity loan using the increased equity in their first home as collateral. They find a new house and use the equity loan as a down payment. Their second house has been chosen in accordance with how much they can earn by renting their first house. They move to the second house and use their rental income, mortgage money, and some additional income to pay both the mortgage on the second house and the equity loan on the first house. They watch *both* these properties appreciate in value. They do this twice more. Finally they retire, sell all the property, and wave goodbye as they sail off on their world cruise!

Arguments often revolve around the amount each teammate is willing to spend on housing. Priorities may differ. Dashed Expectations may arise, manifesting themselves in the Downward Mobility Syndrome. These are the "baby boomers" who expected a mansion and can only afford a "neat little starter house" or "handyman special." Buy it anyway and buy up to the maximum amount you can afford. To help stop those fights regarding affordability, here is some conventional wisdom that may suffice.

There are many rules of thumb for home buying, but they change over the years. A survey shows that the average middle-class,

191

Interest Rates	Monthly Payments	Monthly Income	Annual Income
10%	$438.78	$1,752	$21,024
12%	$514.31	$2,056	$24,672
12¾%	$543.35	$2,172	$26,064
13%	$553.05	$2,212	$26,544
13¼%	$562.87	$2,248	$26,976
13½%	$572.71	$2,288	$27,456
13¾%	$582.66	$2,328	$27,936
14%	$592.44	$2,368	$28,416

middle-income couple spends 35 percent of their gross yearly income on their total housing costs. The old rule was 22 percent. Mortgage markets use a rule of thumb in which the cost of the house should be no more than 250 percent of gross yearly income. Most mortgages cover 80 percent of the purchase price and vary considerably. Another way to look at this is that it should cost 1½ weeks' salary for every month of carrying expenses. The following table shows the income that you might need to qualify for a $50,000 mortgage over a thirty-year period.

Because of inflated costs, you may not get the kind of home of which you have dreamed. Noted financial planner Venita Van Caspel offers the following maximum home purchase prices and relates them to gross annual family income.

Gross Annual Family Income	Maximum Home Purchase Price
$15,000	$36,000 to $43,250
$20,000	$45,000 to $54,000
$25,000	$54,500 to $65,000
$30,000	$64,000 to $76,000
$35,000	$72,750 to $86,750
$40,000	$81,750 to $97,500
$45,000	$91,000 to $108,500
$50,000	$100,000 to $120,000

Notice that she expects the $100,000 to $120,000 home to be purchased by a couple earning at least $50,000. This home may not be much more than the $50,000 home of ten years ago. What does it mean? Should you become "house poor" to achieve the American dream? Perhaps buying a smaller home in a safe area and sending your children to private school is a better alternative for you. (Talking about private school at cocktail parties sounds just as good as talking about the size of your family room.) Don't forget to count hidden expenses such as a gardener, a new roof, rising utility costs, and regular maintenance. Home buying involves more costs than just a mortgage and down payment.

Buying a home also proves the old rule: nature abhors a vacuum. Furniture tends to jump from stores into your living room. This is clearly part of the fun; it is also part of the cost. On the other hand, real estate taxes and interest on the mortgage are tax deductible.

Here's a glossary of mortgage terms that will help you maneuver through the maze.

Fixed-rate mortgage.   Fixed interest rate, usually long term; equal monthly payments of principal and interest until debt is paid in full. Offers stability and long-term tax advantages; limited availability. Interest rates may be higher than other types of financing. New fixed rates are rarely assumable.

Adjustable rate mortgage.   Interest rate changes are based on a financial index, resulting in possible changes in your monthly payments, loan term, and/or principal. Some plans have rate or payment caps. Readily available. Starting interest rate is slightly below market, but payments can increase sharply and frequently if index increases. Payment caps prevent wide fluctuations in payments but may cause negative amortization. Rate caps limit amount total debt can expand.

Renegotiable rate mortgage (rollover).   Interest rate and monthly payments are constant for several years; changes possible thereafter. Long-term mortgage. Less-frequent changes in interest rate offer some stability.

Balloon mortgage.   Monthly payments based on fixed interest

193

rate; usually short term; payments may cover interest only with principal due in full at term end. Offers low monthly payments but possibly no equity until loan is fully paid. When due, loan must be paid off or refinanced. Refinancing poses high risk if rates climb.

Graduated payment mortgage. Lower monthly payments rise gradually (usually over 5 to 10 years), then level off for duration of term. With flexible interest rate, additional payment changes are possible if index changes. Easier to qualify for. Buyer's income must be able to keep pace with scheduled payment increases. With flexible rate, payment increases beyond graduated payments can result in additional negative amortization.

Assumable mortgage. Buyer takes over seller's original, below-market rate mortgage. Lowers monthly payments. May be prohibited if "due on sale" clause is in original mortgage. Not permitted on most new fixed-rate mortgages.

Seller take-back. Seller provides all or part of financing with first or second mortgage. May offer below-market interest rate; may have balloon payment requiring full payment in a few years or refinancing at market rates, which could sharply increase debt.

Buy-down. Developer (or third party) provides interest subsidy that lowers monthly payments during first few years of loan. Can have fixed or flexible interest rate. Offers break from higher payments during early years. Enables buyer with lower income to qualify. With flexible rate mortgage, payments may jump substantially at end of subsidy. Developer may increase selling price.

Choosing a Home with Children in Mind

New parents may not consider residential real estate solely from a financial point of view. For them, residential real estate can reflect a true life need; with a new child there may not be enough room in the old place. One comedian portrays the living room of a family with an eighteen-month-old child by throwing a wash basin filled with toys on the stage. We would like to be able to give children room to grow in an interesting and safe environment. It would be wonderful to give children rooms of their own and perhaps a playroom. There's nothing wrong with a backyard, either, and a sandbox or swing makes for more fun.

The need to move to accommodate children has been much exaggerated, however. Many years ago, I took a decorating course and enjoyed working with the instructor on the homes of various people. One was that of a couple with a small city apartment. Expecting a second child, they were going crazy trying to find enough money to move. It was gratifying to rework the walls of that small Manhattan apartment so that it could accommodate a second child. As far as I know, the couple never moved and never regretted it.

My point is that it can be a mistake to move merely because a child is coming into the family. Even though this chapter discusses how to select a home, what to pay, how to finance it, and how to approach a home closing, don't lose sight of the fact that the most worthwhile alternative may be remaining where you are.

This possibility can be a shock to new parents. They little appreciate how quickly their children will grow through various stages. Toddlerhood comes and goes before you know it. Once the children are ready for school, you may wish you had selected a home (even if it was a little small) in a neighborhood with a better school system. If you move to a better school district, you may be sorry that you did not move to a neighborhood with a great many schoolchildren, because the commute between friends' homes is too long. By the time this has been resolved with a third move, the children will enter adolescence and have one desire: to become independent of you and their surroundings. Now you may wish you had provided opportunities for a safe but independent environment outside the home. Should you find such a place and move again, the kids will be ready for college. They'll leave home. That is, if everybody is lucky. By now, you'll be ready to move and close up the empty nest.

This fantasy trip through moving for the sake of the kids illustrates the point that children should not be a primary considera-

195

tion in moving. Once you have decided to move for other reasons, consider the children in selecting a new residence.

Factors to look for in a child-oriented residence are:

- The quality of schools in the area
- The number of children in the classroom
- The student/teacher ratio
- The quality of textbooks
- The availability of computer equipment
- The status and background of the principal
- The comparative reading scores of the school (the local board of education should have this information, since a good school system keeps such records)
- The age of the schools
- Safety in the area
- Number of crossing guards
- The proximity of parks, libraries, and religious institutions
- The commute to museums and other cultural centers
- Traffic patterns, including those caused by industrial parks in the area
- The time taken from your children because of your commute to work

Step 9: Housing Task Synopsis

- Resolve to buy despite real estate phobia
- Investigate mortgages
- Calculate your borrowing power
- Prioritize your needs
- Search for neighborhoods and investigate specific property
- Remake the Pay Yourself First Budget to test various expenditure scenarios
- Buy a residence

STEP 10: TAX PLANNING

Taxes can be a feuding couple's best friend. The government is always a good scapegoat for interpersonal tensions. The kings and queens of France and England knew that, and kept rebellions down for centuries by keeping up the European wars. The minute they stopped, the revolutions came.

Every divorce mediator knows how to use tax planning when couples get steaming mad. Just bring up the government and let them each redirect their anger toward a third party. You can do this in your home, too. Remember, tax avoidance is not a crime, it is a national pastime. There is nothing wrong with the two of you working together for a common goal—tax savings.

The interesting thing about the tax savings game is that periodically Uncle Sam changes the rules, usually under the guise of a so-called simplified tax act. It keeps tax lawyers busy, and it can keep you and your teammate united in purpose. Making you a tax expert, however, is not my goal. Instead, I would like you to acknowledge tax planning and bear tax consequences in mind as you make financial decisions during the course of the year. April 14 is not the time to start your tax planning (unless it's for the year ahead).

To do this you must make a "working tax chart" and refresh your memory about tax rules as you make important decisions. Eventually, you will have enough familiarity with the rules to meet efficiently with an accountant or tax planner. As with investments, you are urged to rely on the advice of experts, but only after you have at least a nodding acquaintance with individual taxation.

How do you view taxes? Some people just pay them; they have no desire to work at saving taxes. Many wealthy people do not take advantage of tax loopholes. Other people pay taxes reluctantly and work at saving taxes with a passion. Oddly enough, I had two low-income clients who were heavily audited because they participated in a scheme to take massive tax deductions by incorporating as a so-called religious institution. They paid $6,000 to a fraudulent "church" for the privilege of saving taxes even though they were in low brackets. Why do otherwise honest, hardworking people get into so much trouble with the IRS? Perhaps the government seems so impersonal that morality is no longer an issue. Perhaps the inability to budget is so ingrained that they cannot pay the tax. But probably it is because of a complete ignorance of legitimate ways to avoid, not evade, taxes. Before we go further, take the following silent survey.

Silent Survey #11

Think about the following questions:

Are you in mortal fear of an audit?

Do you have a guilty tax secret you'd like to share with an expert to get advice?

Do you believe that tax avoidance is immoral, even if legal?

Do you believe that paying even one extra tax dollar is a mistake to be avoided?

Are you prepared to keep scrupulous records of receipts and other tax documentations?

Are you prepared to share all economic data with your teammate so all financial aspects of your tax return are revealed?

Are you prepared to learn about all economic data from your teammate so all financial aspects of your tax returns are known to you?

Is tax planning and preparation your task? Your teammate's task? A joint task?

Do you enjoy, dislike, or feel neutral about learning the tax aspects of personal finance?

This survey brings you far in judging task allocation, attitudes toward taxes, and priority of tax planning, and even touches on

PERSONAL TAX CONSEQUENCE CHART

Type of Tax Incurred	State or Federal	State Tax Bracket	Federal Tax Bracket	Amount of Tax or Deduction	Comments or Strategies for Minimizing or Maximizing	When Payment or Savings Will Occur	Type of Deduction or Credit
Income							Real estate tax deduction
							Interest payment deduction
Estate							Business expense
							Other (see Appendix)
Gift							Depreciation
							Child care deduction
Sales							Investment tax credit
							Other tax credit
Other							Exemption for dependent
							person
							person
							person

feelings of civic duty. To get a head start on this year's tax returns:

- Check your filing system for a deductible receipt file.
- Determine your best filing status.
- Take your prior returns to an accountant after April 15 and have him/her recheck them for better planning this year.
- Open your IRA and fund it as soon as possible. In many cases it is still tax deductible; in every case the income is tax deferred.
- Allocate record-keeping tasks between you.
- Keep a Personal Tax Consequence chart. Make entries for those events you can predict (e.g., selling your house), then keep it regularly throughout the year.
- See your advisor for a tax strategy for those significant taxes.
- Use your Cash Flow Calendar to note when taxes must be paid or refunds are expected.
- Use the Pay Yourself First Budget to save enough in a liquid fund—e.g., money market or short-term CD—to pay taxes when due.

Step 10: Tax Planning Task Synopsis

- Note your filing status and tax bracket.
- Improve your filing system.
- Keep the tax chart up to date.

8

The Money Questions
Most Often Asked
by Couples

THIS chapter answers the twenty questions most often asked about team money management. The questions fall into four categories: (1) In Whose Name Should We Own Assets and Incur Liabilities? (2) Methods of Setting Goals and Meeting Expectations; (3) Spousal Rights and Liability; and (4) General Money Management.

IN WHOSE NAME SHOULD WE OWN
ASSETS AND INCUR LIABILITIES?

1. *Should we have joint or separate savings bank accounts?*
   The best answer to this is both. Joint savings bank accounts, joint brokerage accounts, and other joint investment vehicles give a feeling of trust and of doing things together. They also give each

party full access to the team money. In fact, if anything should happen to one of you, the other will automatically inherit the funds in any type of joint account. However, as long as each of you knows what the other has in their separate accounts, and separateness does not necessarily lead to secretiveness, there is nothing wrong with separate accounts. If you use separate accounts, however, make sure that you have your estate affairs in order, perhaps with a power of attorney making clear that the other party has the right to obtain separate funds if the owner becomes incapacitated.

2. Should we have separate credit cards?

The two of you should have separate credit cards so that you establish separate credit identities. If both of you have established credit records, it will be easier to obtain good loans. At the same time, if one of you has established a poor credit rating because of bad money management, the other will stay "clean." What you must do, however, is keep your credit management under control so that the two of you as a team do not overburden yourselves with too much debt service. By using good record keeping and good boardroom techniques, you should be able to do so even though you have several credit cards.

3. Should we have joint or separate checking accounts?

Separate checking accounts are better. This means that each partner will retain the autonomy needed in any money-making relationship. It means that both of you will have some money to spend and to manage without the immediate knowledge and consent of the other. It also means that you will both have some responsibility for managing money and will avoid overdrawing your checking account because you have not had time to consult with the other. This does not mean that you should not also establish a joint account from which you will pay all joint bills or business expenses. If you have entirely separate accounts, then you must keep your records together and available to each other.

4. What name should be on our lease or deed?

If both of you are to be the beneficial owners of property or the beneficial occupants of a leasehold, both names should be on the property, the deed, or the lease. With respect to a deed, this will mean automatic inheritance of the real estate by one partner if the other dies. If you are not a married couple, the deed will have to have both names on it and specifically state that it is taken as "joint tenants with right of survivorship." This happens automatically if you are husband and wife. With respect to a leasehold, if one of you leaves or dies, the other one will be left virtually out in the cold if their name is not also on the lease. Those with a special problem with creditors who might attach property may want to treat the matter differently because of these circumstances.

GOALS AND EXPECTATIONS

5. How should we set up a college fund?

Before the new tax law of 1987, a Clifford Trust was the best method of setting up a college fund. Its purpose was to shift income taxes from the parent to the child's lower tax bracket by putting the money in the child's name in trust. It also allowed the parents to receive the principal back after ten years, although the income derived from investments belonged to the child. With the new 1987 tax law, this income-shifting device is no longer available. Nevertheless, the first $500 of income received in the child's name is tax free, and the second $500 is taxable at the child's lower rate. Therefore, you might want to create a trust for the child's education. If the trust is irrevocable it will not be counted in your estate for estate tax purposes if one of the parents should die. If it's revocable, it will be counted. In either case, under the new tax law most of the income will be taxed at the parents' higher rate. Nevertheless, the spirit of the thing—segregating untouchable funds for a specific goal—is best achieved through setting up a trust.

Remember, however, that only the first $1,000 of yearly income will have a tax advantage. The rest of the income will be taxed at your marginal rate.

6. *Will an annuity help us with our retirement goal?*

An annuity is useful when you no longer can fund any deferred tax plan. An IRA, Keogh, or employee benefit plan permits you to invest money and defer taxes until such time as you retire and withdraw the funds. However, all three programs are limited in the amount that you can contribute. If you have funded these sources to the limit, only then use an annuity. They will give you tax-deferred money. Shop carefully and compare these products.

7. *How can I financially protect children of a first marriage without interfering with the good feelings of my second marriage?*

In almost every state you and your spouse can sign a prenuptial agreement (signed either before or after the marriage) in which your spouse waives any rights in your estate. Most states automatically give one-third to a spouse for their share even if you do not leave such a sum in your will. With a prenuptial agreement, the second spouse waives those rights, leaving you free to make a will devoted entirely to your children. However, I do not find that this makes for good feelings in second marriages unless both parties want them and both parties have children they wish to protect. When this is not the case, a second spouse should receive some gift under a will. If an estate is small you might wish to have your spouse waive their one-third right but leave at least 20 percent to them. If you want to increase the protection that your children have after your death without causing hard feelings in your relationship, the only answer is insurance. Second spouses rarely mind that a heavy policy has been taken out with children of a first marriage as beneficiaries, even when the premiums are a little steep.

8. *What's the best overall retirement program if my spouse is an entrepreneur?*

If your long-range planning shows you can put $20,000 or less a year into a retirement account for the self-employed, use a Keogh account. Under Keogh, you will have to provide employee benefits for certain of your employees who have been with you for a period of time. However, apart from this, Keoghs are generally *self-directed,* meaning that all investment decisions can be made by the entrepreneur. Once you find that your business has prospered to the extent that more money could be contributed for retirement, the best thing to do is speak to a pension planner and attorney about incorporating so that you can provide a corporate pension plan. These plans permit you to put a greater percentage of your draw into your pension but also imposes a heavier responsibility to distribute sums to employees.

9. *How much and what kind of insurance should we have to manage risk properly?*

Everyone should have enough term life insurance to meet the needs of their dependents; there is no need to purchase insurance for independent spouses or adult children, although you may wish to do so just to build your estate. On the other hand, when there are small children or a dependent spouse, it is absolutely essential to provide death benefits equal to at least ten years of your after-tax salary. In addition, everyone should have as full insurance as possible covering the cost of their home and irreplaceable valuables. Where available, enough disability insurance to cover at least three-quarters of your overhead if you cannot work is recommended. Disability insurance can be costly; therefore, you should have at least three months of hurdle money and buy a policy that does not begin to give benefits until ninety days have passed. You'll find that this greatly reduces the cost of the policy.

10. *Is there a financially sane way to take a trip around the world, buy a boat, or get another extravagant luxury?*

The Pay Yourself First Budget is the answer to luxury planning.

205

It is my personal philosophy that no one should give up any dream. You may, however, have to take a little longer than hoped to achieve it. But good steady planning and inclusion of the luxury item in the Pay Yourself First Budget will do it. It is often appropriate if the item is a once-in-a-lifetime matter that debt be incurred, with the couple planning to pay back that debt steadily after they have incurred it to enjoy their special luxury.

11. *When is a couple financially ready to have children?*
Never, but that shouldn't stop them from having children anyway. Having children is a sweeping change in a relationship, and no one can ever be totally financially prepared for what can happen. For example, even after the best planning, the wife may find that she has become physically ill and cannot work. Instead of expecting perfect planning, expect to be able to roll with the punches.

SPOUSAL RIGHTS AND LIABILITY

12. *What are my rights under my spouse's pension plan?*
Every pension plan differs. The only way to answer this question is to speak to the personnel officer at your spouse's company. Most plans permit a surviving spouse to receive funds at the same or reduced rate for the rest of their life. Others offer a death benefit option—a lump sum in lieu of yearly amounts.

13. *What are my rights under the law with respect to spousal inheritance?*
Every state has a spousal elective share. The amount is usually one-third. Many states have what is known as dower and courtesy; this old-fashioned concept has been translated in many ways, but often means that the spouse inherits the marital home. If a will is left leaving less than the spousal elective share, the spouse could legally challenge the will and obtain statutory rights. If no will has been left, the law of intestacy applies. This means that a

second statute, which sets forth what each person (depending on their degree of kinship to the deceased) will receive, dictates inheritance rights. In most states a spouse will receive at least half an estate if there are children.

14. *What is my liability for a joint tax return?*

A joint tax return that both of you have signed makes you jointly and severally (meaning together with your spouse and separately from him or her) liable to the government for the amounts. If your spouse prepared the account and actually perpetrated a fraud, you can plead innocence. This becomes a matter of fact and proof. You would be much better off not closing your eyes to the issue of tax preparation and insisting on understanding your tax picture and the tax computation.

GENERAL MONEY MANAGEMENT

15. *What's the most efficient way to pay bills?*

There are three efficient ways to pay bills, each with its own pros and cons. The first is to keep a good Pay Yourself First Budget and use a joint checking account in which you have deposited sufficient sums to cover your expenses. In this way you will have canceled checks as receipts for payment and evidence for tax deductions if any of the bills are deductible items.

A second efficient method that appeals to some people whose income is erratic and who have to plan very carefully is to take a monthly cash advance on a credit card, use those funds to pay bills (also by check), and pay the credit card amount immediately upon receipt of that bill. This allows the couple (particularly the young person who may start their financial planning a few hundred dollars behind and need some type of immediate help) to be always one month in arrears without incurring any penalties or any charges. Remember that cash advances are at best limited to $500, and if bill paying on a monthly basis exceeds that amount, as it does with most older couples, this bill-paying method cannot work.

The third and most revolutionary way of paying bills is through automated bill-paying accounts with banks. Its major drawback is that the system is still in its infancy, and it may be difficult to find a bank that provides this service. If there is one in your location, check the charges; they may be prohibitive.

16. *What do stockbrokers, accountants, and trustees really charge?*

For the most part, stockbrokers charge on a commission basis. A normal charge per $10,000 worth of individual stock is $500 to $1,000; per $10,000 of bond purchase the fee would be $100 to $600; and you can expect to spend $400 to $850 on commissions if you buy a load commission mutual fund. Accountants generally charge by the hour, and that differs considerably in urban, suburban, and rural areas. The only way to find this out is to ask. Every accountant (and attorney) will differentiate between the fees charged for the senior partner, junior partner, and bookkeeping assistant. Trustees charge a statutory fee set by the state in which the trust has been created and under which the trustee is functioning. Average trust fees are 3 percent of the money handled.

17. *Is there a recommended will for a couple with children?*

While there is never any will that fits everyone, a will for a young couple with children usually sets forth the following:

- Revocation of prior wills
- Payment of debts and administrative expenses
- Personal property with insurance policy to surviving spouse
- Income to spouse in trust for life, remainder to children of first $600,000
- Remainder to spouse or to children if spouse predeceases
- A trust for children to receive income only until they reach age thirty (most favored age)

18. *If my spouse and I sell our home, what are the tax implications?*

Under the new tax law there is no longer any capital gain, but all profits from the sale of a house, including a marital residence, is taxed as ordinary income. If, however, you and your spouse purchase a new primary residence within twenty-four months of the sale, any profit that you have plowed back into the new purchase will not be counted as taxable. In addition, if you or your spouse are over the age of fifty-five at the time the sale is made, the first $125,000 of profit is exempt from tax even if you don't plow it back into a new residence.

19. *How will I manage money if my spouse becomes ill or incapacitated?*

Every one of you should have a durable power of attorney. This gives you the power to handle separate funds in the name of your spouse, or their share of any joint funds, even though they are ill and cannot sign checks, make decisions, or are even mentally incapacitated. Remember that a power of attorney ceases to be effective after the death of a spouse. When that happens, your estate plan comes into effect. For that to work there must be at least some hurdle money that you can use until probate or estate distribution has been completed. Sometimes immediate receipt of insurance funds is the best answer, together with your own separate account.

20. *What's the most efficient way to make joint burial arrangements, donate body parts, and control extraordinary medical treatments so as to cause my spouse the least possible pain in the time of grief?*

A living will is acceptable in many states and dictates how a spouse wishes medical treatment to be administered.

Notes

[1] Jürg Willi, *Couples in Collusion* (Claremont, CA: Hunter House), page 149.

[2] Willi, *Couples in Collusion*, page 151.

[3] Ibid, page 163.

For Further Reading

ACKERMAN, DIANE LEIGHTON. *The Only Guide You'll Ever Need to Marry Money.* Simon & Schuster, 1982. Pretty silly, but good escapist reading for when you're feeling under stress.

BARSOTTI, C. *Kings Don't Carry Money.* Dodd Mead, 1981. Another short and humorous book about money and why controlling it is so hard for us.

BERG, ADRIANE G. *Moneythink.* Pilgrim Press, 1980. A clear, simple overview of your associations with money and how they affect your financial planning style.
———. *Your Kids, Your Money.* Prentice Hall, 1981. My own book on kids, college, insurance, and inheritance.
———. *Your Wealth-Building Years: The Secrets of Money Management for 21- to 35-Year-Olds.* Newmarket Press, 1986.

All the secrets of money management for those in this age group earning $16,000 or more per year.

BLOCH, SONNY & GRACE LICHTENSTEIN. *Sonny Bloch's Inside Real Estate: The Complete Guide to Buying & Selling Your Home, Co-Op or Condominium.* Weidenfeld & Nicholson, 1987. A new standard work for the "average man" by real-estate guru Bloch. Should already be on your shelf.

BOCKL, GEORGE. *How to Use Leverage to Make Money in Local Real Estate.* Reward Books/Prentice Hall, 1965. Fast-talking hustler tells how the made a bundle in *terra firma.* Don't believe all his war stories, but you can learn a lot from this good job of explaining leverage.

BOLLES, RICHARD NELSON. *What Color is Your Parachute?* Ten Speed Press, 1988 (updated regularly). A classic for individuals and couples whose problems stem from unhappiness with their occupation(s). Great for the Dashed Expectations crowd.

BORNEMAN, ERNEST. *The Psychoanalysis of Money.* Urizen, 1976. A revealing, if technical, look at how our behavior and attitudes toward money are formed.

DUNNAN, NANCY. *Dun and Bradstreet's Guide to Your Investments, 1987.* Harper & Row, 1987. Contains detailed information about, and analyses of, every aspect of every investment opportunity you're likely to encounter.

JANDA, LOUIS. *How to Live With an Imperfect Person.* New American Library, 1985. Will help you cope with your spouse's (and sometimes, perhaps, with your own) shortcomings.

LESHAN, LAWRENCE. *How to Meditate: A Guide to Self-Discovery.* Bantam Books, 1986. A Western approach to relaxation, and great for practicing before or after the boardroom meetings.

LITTLE, JEFFREY B. and LUCIEN RHODES. *Understanding Wall Street*, 2nd edition. Liberty House/TAB Books, 1987. Great for anyone interested in mastering the fundamentals of capitalism.

MYER, JOHN M. *Understanding Financial Statements: What the Executive Should Know About the Accountant's Statements.* New American Library, 1968. A must, particularly for the "helpless" Doll's House partner.

NELSON, WAYNE F. *Extraordinary Investments for Ordinary Investors: Choosing the Best from the New Money Packages.* Putnam, 1985. A solid, up-to-date study of mutual funds and much more. Current and complete.

NIERENBERG, GERARD. *The Art of Negotiating.* Cornerstone Books/Simon & Schuster, 1984. A good choice if you're wondering why you always lose.

SCHWARTZ, ROBERT. *The Home Owner's Legal Guide.* Collier/Macmillan, 1977. What to do before you get to the closing.

SPOONER, JOHN D. *Sex & Money: Behind the Scenes With the Big-Time Brokers.* Houghton Mifflin, 1985. An intriguing analysis of sex and Wall Street money.

WITKIN-LANOIL, GEORGIA, PH.D. *The Female Stress Syndrome: How to Recognize and Live With It.* Newmarket Press, 1984. ———. *The Male Stress Syndrome: How to Recognize and Live With It.* Newmarket Press, 1986. The titles tell it all. Practical, do-it-yourself ways to measure and deal with that incapacitating tension.

TAXES AND TAX GUIDES. What can I tell you? All the large paperback compendiums are good and fairly interchangeable. You should have at least one. (For example, there's Price Water-house, Lasser, H&R Block, Arthur Anderson, and many more.)

"MONEY PAPER." Edited by Vita Nelson. This is the only newsletter endorsed by the author. It contains an incredible number of useful tips and strategies on taxes, retirement, and even stock investment plans. For a free copy, write to Bochner & Berg, 200 Park Avenue South, New York, NY 10003.

Index

About the Author

Adriane G. Berg is the author of *Moneythink, Your Kids, Your Money,* and *Your Wealth-building Years.* A co-founder of the financial planning firm of Berg & Montag Associates, she is chair of the New York State Bar Association in Estate Planning, and is on the Board of Directors of the New York Chapter of the International Association for Financial Planning. She teaches at the New School for Social Research, conducts frequent seminars for banks and professional groups, and hosts her own radio show on WMCA in New York. She lives in New York City.